THE LAST JEWS
OF KERALA

ALSO BY THE SAME AUTHOR

Holy Warriors

THE LAST JEWS
OF KERALA

The 2000-Year History of India's
Forgotten Jewish Community

EDNA FERNANDES

Skyhorse Publishing

Skyhorse Publishing books may be purchased in bulk at special discounts for sales promotion, corporate gifts, fund-raising, or educational purposes. Special editions can also be created to specifications. For details, contact the Special Sales Department, Skyhorse Publishing, 307 West 36th Street, 11th Floor, New York, NY 10018 or info@skyhorsepublishing.com.

Skyhorse® and Skyhorse Publishing® are registered trademarks of Skyhorse Publishing, Inc.®, a Delaware corporation.

Visit our website at www.skyhorsepublishing.com.

10 9 8 7 6 5 4 3 2 1

Library of Congress Cataloging-in-Publication data

Fernandes, Edna.
The Last Jews of Kerala: The Two Thousand year History of India's Forgotten Jewish Community by Edna Fernandes
     p. cm.
ISBN 978-1-60239-267-0 (hardcover)
ISBN 978-1-63450-271-9 (paperback)
ISBN 978-1-62636-935-1 (ebook)

Printed in the United States of America

To Felix, with love.

CONTENTS

INTRODUCTION

"Our Days Are Like Passing Shadows."

—PSALM 144:4, INSCRIPTION ON THE PARADESI SYNAGOGUE
CLOCKTOWER IN JEW TOWN, MATTANCHERRY

The last of the summer monsoon rains had passed. Bruised grey skies and merciless sheets of black rain yielded to freshly-washed vistas of blue and green. Coconut palms sashayed in breezes that blew inland from the Arabian Sea, bearing the taste of salt and smell of fish. Jackfruit and papaya trees shimmered in the sunlight as crows feasted on fruits shed onto the grass below, beaks disgorging seeds and bleeding sweet dark juices into the soil. As the humidity rose, jewel-like flowers of pink and red drooped from branches that encircled the cemetery stone walls. Cochin had burst into renewed life.

Skin slick with sweat, the gravediggers completed their task and gathered up the shovels to withdraw before the funeral. With their departure, only the parakeets were left to pay their respects from a vantage point high in the palms overlooking the old Jewish cemetery, yellow eyes transfixed by the mawkish scene below.

It was September 2006, the burial day for Shalom Cohen, last of the priestly line of *kohanim* in Cochin and one of the dwindling Diaspora tribe known as the White Jews of Kerala. With his death, just twelve remained. An ambulance stopped at the gates of the cemetery, followed by a group of mourners dressed in spotless white. In keeping with Cochini custom, Psalm 91 was sung to relinquish custody of the body to God:

"No disaster shall befall you,
No calamity shall come upon your home.
For He has charged his angels
To guard you wherever you go,
To lift you on their hands
For fear you should strike your foot against a stone.
You shall step on asp and cobra,
You shall tread safely on snake and serpent."

The last of the White Jews chanted their lamentations as they approached the graveside, faces the same color as their vestments, hands raised in supplication to indifferent blue skies. Shalom's body had been purified through the cleansing ritual before being dressed in a simple white shroud. Earth from Jerusalem and from Cranganore, the ancient Jewish kingdom of Kerala, was placed in his eyes and mouth. His head was swathed in strips of white linen, his corpse sprinkled with rose water, an old Sephardic custom, and then he was laid in a wooden coffin bereft of all adornment.

The coffin was carried on a palanquin by bearers to the site of the grave, the procession stopping seven times along the way to mark the seven references to the word "vanity" in Ecclesiastes. Winds rushed through the towering palms, their treetops bowed as if in deference to the occasion. As the parakeets sang their own plaintive tribute, the coffin was lowered into the ground, entombed within the red earth. Once the ceremonials had been completed, the bereaved left the graveside throwing fistfuls of dust and torn grass over their shoulders to symbolize the tearing of their hearts. The funeral had shaken this tiny community, which is all that remains of a once splendid history that crossed centuries and continents. To those present, it had been a terrible epiphany: with the death of Shalom, the demise of the last Jews of Kerala no longer seemed an event fixed far into an intangible future, but an inevitability with shape and form, casting its promise of foreboding upon them all.

* * * *

I came across the Jews of Cochin on my first visit to Kerala in 2002. While working on a story about tea plantations I chanced upon Synagogue Lane, home to a diminishing group of white-skinned Indian Jews who claimed a lineage dating back to the era of Solomon.

Then, as now, they were defensive, introspective and wary of strangers to the point of paranoia. The White or Paradesi Jews claimed they were both the only Jewish community remaining in the whole of Kerala and the Jewish community with the oldest history in India. In many ways they were typically Indian, yet they retained an ethnic and cultural distinction that was unmistakable. The men and women wore sparkling white *lunghis* and *saris*, ate Jewish-Indian food with their hands, even adapted some of the Hindu customs to their way of life, but they remained orthodox in their Jewish beliefs, and their fair skin made for an arresting contrast to the polished ebony complexion of the Keralites. In gleaming garments they wandered through Jew Town like ghosts communing with the living. Back in 2002, the elders still harbored hopes of saving the future generations by pressuring the last young Jew and Jewess among them to marry, deploying the most devastating of weapons in their arsenal of persuasion: guilt, on an apocalyptic scale. "Marry, bear a child. Or the end of thousands of years of Jewish history rests on *your* heads," they told the youngsters. The brinkmanship failed and the fate of the White Jews was sealed.

Within the mosaic of histories of the subcontinent, theirs is a story easily overlooked and yet the Kerala Jews remained indelibly fixed in my mind: a people who vanquished the treacheries of history, fled Israel after the destruction of the beloved Second Temple and later escaped the horrors of the Inquisition in Europe to build a new life in India. Then, when all seemed safe, when they felt assured they were beyond the grasp of extinction, circumstance delivered them to danger once again. What is it like for a people whose end has come?

Imagine if one had been able to witness the end days with the people of Easter Island, the Mayans of Central America or others whose civilizations suffered such precipitous downfalls, leaving behind ruined temples as inadequate tributes to what once was. In the book *Collapse: How Societies Choose to Fail or Survive*, Jared Diamond writes of such civilizations, how they often wittingly contributed to their own disastrous decline and how the evocative ruins they left behind continue to mesmerize us: "We marvel at them when as children we first learn of them through pictures. When we grow up, many of us plan vacations in order to experience them firsthand as tourists," he said. "We feel drawn to their often spectacular and haunting beauty and also to the mysteries they pose."

Such mysteries as did they know they were courting destruction and if so why did they continue? Their ruins are not mere archaeology, but warnings that cry out from the past, symbols of societies that once seemed invincible and yet precipitated their own demise. As I walked amidst the ruined synagogues in Cochin or even down Synagogue Lane, thronging with Nikon-toting tourists, evidently these were not grand temples marking a mighty civilization. Yet on a very modest scale, they were the poignant remains of a nonetheless remarkable and ancient people who dated back to the era of the First Temple, according to their oral history.

They had survived the worst that could be thrown at them—tyranny, dispossession of a nation, the razing of their seat of worship—and yet endured to refashion their community amid the tamarind trees and jasmine blossoms of India. Unlike Diaspora elsewhere in the world during history, the Jews of Kerala were a feted people, embraced by neighbors of all creeds. While other faiths in India were susceptible to the sinister seductions of communal violence, the Jews of Kerala remained immune to the troubles that periodically threatened to endanger India's delicately-poised religious equilibrium. Part of the reason for this was sheer lack of numbers: they were simply too small in number, too insignificant a lobby to be perceived as a threat to Hindu, Muslim or Christian. They were never a proselytizing people but cultural chameleons who adapted easily. Over the centuries they proved to be exceptionally adept at surviving the volatile shifts in the political order of the region, from the Cochini royal dynasty to the Portuguese, Dutch and British invading colonial powers.

Despite every advantage, in the end they were undone not by anti-Semitism or war, nor pestilence or the vagaries of nature, but at the hands of one another as they allowed dissent and rivalry to breed within their ranks. That divide was institutionalized in apartheid between Jews of different skin color in Kerala and meant there were ultimately too few marriages, too few children and, therefore, no future. When the state of Israel beckoned in 1948, many answered its call and left behind a redundant few.

Like other lost societies, today's visitors to Cochin are also lured by the romance and longevity of this history and as they take their snapshots, one can see that the Jews of Kerala have already become a souvenir people. Soon their story will also be immortalized on key-rings and other collector's items. Already, we are within the epilogue of one of the great stories of the Jewish Diaspora, an epic which will end in Kerala in our lifetime, perhaps within a decade.

For these reasons, I went back in the autumn of 2006. I was pregnant with my son at the time, which made me particularly attuned to the sensitivities of a community that had not celebrated a birth for decades. On my return, I discovered that the White Jews were not in fact the only Jewry left in Kerala. There was another equally small community across the waters called the Black Jews. The Black, or Malabari Jews as they were also known, was a distinct group that lived in the main town of Ernakulam, as well as the nearby villages of Chennamangalam, Mala and Parul, which are all within a few kilometers. They were known as the "Black" Jews because of their darker coloring, which was the same as that of the indigenous Keralites, a skin color that told its own tale of historical integration with the Indians and marriage to converts to Judaism.

The two sides, the Blacks and Whites, had suffered a bitter feud for centuries, their relations marked by apartheid, discrimination, claim and counter-claim over who arrived first in India, who could claim common ancestry with the Jewish founding fathers of the subcontinent and who could lay claim to religious purity. In Hindu-dominated India, a country where purity is paramount and bestows ascendancy in the social hierarchy as well as political and economic privilege, these were not petty concerns but the very foundation of one's survival. The stakes were high and history showed that neither side—Black or White—was willing to relinquish their claim. *This* lay at the heart of the split within the Jewish community, evident for the last four centuries, polarizing them when there should have been much more to unite them. It also proved to be their undoing in the end.

Where together they once numbered in the thousands, with eight synagogues and vast estates of plantations and houses that stretched across the tropical coastal plains of Cochin, today there are fewer than fifty Jews, and just one working synagogue remains with not enough men to form the quorum needed for prayer on Sabbath. The other synagogues have fallen into disuse, crumbling into dust, annexed by jungle and home to nests of cobras.

The story takes us on a voyage from King Solomon's Israel to the west coast of modern-day India, moving between the great intercontinental migrations of early modern history and the tragicomic feud of Jew Town that has brought Kerala's Jewry to its knees. At its heart is the battle for racial equality in the backwaters of India, an ancient civil rights movement which fought segregation in the synagogue, that began in the sixteenth century yet succeeded too late to save its people.

This is the end of history for the Jews of Kerala. Sixty years after the formation of the state of Israel, sixty years after the birth of the Indian republic, the clock is ticking for India's oldest Jewish Diaspora, and it is one minute to midnight.

* * * *

So how did it begin? The available history is a patchwork of folklore, fable and historical fact. The Old Testament indicates that the first Jews landed on Indian shores thousands of years ago, sailing from Israel on trade missions from the court of King Solomon. Biblical accounts depict sailors and merchants docking at Kerala's main harbor, charged with procuring spices and exotic treasure such as "elephant's tooth, peacocks and apes". A further wave of immigrants arrived after the Roman capture of Jerusalem and destruction of the Second Temple in 70 CE, a ruthless act of conquest which sent the Jews into exile, scattering their tribes across the globe like seeds of last hope to the winds.

This particular Diaspora never knew persecution in their adopted land. Instead, they were feted by Kerala's rajas as foreign kings, lavished with land, privilege and autonomy. In return for privileges that included respect for the Sabbath, the right to use symbols of royalty such as parasols and gun salutes as well as protection from hostile invader forces, the Jews swore fealty to the Cochini rajas, fighting alongside their armies during battles with warring neighbors and acting as advisers at court. They were respected both on the battlefield and in the trading bazaar, seen as both valiant soldiers and astute merchants. As the turbaned raja held audiences in his chamber, seated aloft his silver throne or silk-upholstered day bed as the *pankah-wallah* gently fanned the regal presence, the Jews were periodically summoned, heads inclined in supplication, to this inner sanctum. The king would receive them in his palace in Mattancherry, which lies adjacent to the Paradesi Synagogue, evidence itself of the proximity of the Jews to their patron's heart. The land on which the Paradesi synagogue and Jew Town were built was provided by the raja, a safe haven when they were driven out from their first city Cranganore. As a trading people, as people of letters and languages, through the centuries they stayed close to Kerala's kings until India's princely states finally ceded control to the Republic of India on Independence Day in 1947.

Yet more than two millennia since trade routes and the fall of Jerusalem first brought the settlers to seek sanctuary in these lands, this once illustrious people is now in its final days. To understand how, I began at the end, among the remaining White Jews of Synagogue Lane in Mattancherry and the Black Jews of Ernakulam's Jew Town.

The district of Cochin is comprised of Ernakulam, the nearest thing to a big city which lies on the mainland's coast and is less than an hour's drive from the southern peninsula of Fort Cochin, and Mattancherry. Mattancherry also had its own Jew Town once, but today the community is confined to just a cluster of houses on a single street, with the rest of the village inhabited by Christians, Muslims and Hindus who bought up the Jewish homes piecemeal as the Paradesi community emigrated or died out. Separated by a rancorous past and a stretch of swamp-like water that crisscrosses the low-lying land and canals, the Black and White Jews have been compelled to come together in these final days.

This account—a mixture of interview and confession, archive and diary—charts their rise and fall, from a glorious centuries-long heyday when they were the confidantes of kings, to the twentieth-century decline and twenty-first-century denouement. Their fortunes were undone by a devastating nexus of apartheid, centuries of inter-breeding, mental illness and a latter-day exodus from Kerala after the creation of Israel in 1948.

This exodus proved to be a revival of sorts in the fortunes for the Kerala Jews in Israel. In returning to the place where it began, the narrative seemed to have come full circle, providing an ostensibly poetic conclusion for those who chose Israel over India. The majority were sent to live in the Negev. It proved to be a shocking adjustment: exchanging verdant south India for the barren beauty of the desert; a timeless and orthodox Jewish way of life for a secular and increasingly Westernized one; the security and ancient tolerance of Kerala for a life refracted through the deadly prism of the Arab-Israeli conflict.

A few faltered as a result of change, withering once transplanted from their natural setting. Others thrived on the mighty challenge of Zionism, of making the desert of Abraham bloom once more. Akin to some Biblical parable, they grew roses and gladioli in the desert and initiated what was to become a major Israeli industry: horticultural exports. But perhaps, even more miraculous, family life prospered again as Cochini Jews married and raised children. In Israel at least, life has returned for the Kerala Jews.

Yet as thousands made the *aliyah*, deserting one paradise for what they hoped would be another, those in India have become a people cursed by no marriages, only funerals. They are the old and the unmarried, the embodiment of an exhausted history. These twelve White Jews and thirty Black Jews scattered across Cochin are reconciled to play out the final scene in India, rather than Israel.

Among them is Gamy Salem, the sole living descendant of a "Jewish Gandhi", Abraham Barak Salem, a contemporary of both the Mahatma and Jawaharlal Nehru, who eschewed national politics to lead the civil rights battle for equality in the synagogue and bring these estranged brothers into belated union. Then there is the romantic saga of the young lovers, Balfour and Baby, the first Black and White Jews who defied the elders to marry; Sarah, a widowed White Jewess who is the remaining Kerala heir to the Cohen name, which once bore the blood of the priestly line and who must now survive the cunning machinations of her Muslim and Christian hangers-on as they plot to inherit her wealth. Babu, the gentle aquarium-keeper tasked with conducting the ritual kosher slaughter of chickens, also has his place as the last *shohet*.

Perhaps the most evocative of all is the plight of the youngest members who cannot, or will not, marry. Anil, a twenty-something Black Jew, longs for "a Jewish wife who will not give me headache". Now he must decide—marry outside his people or abandon the land he loves to find a bride. Yaheh is the youngest of the White Jews, who spends her days selling two-rupee tickets to tourists at the synagogue and her nights patting her pet dog Baby Doll. For more than a decade, Yaheh and her cousin Keith suffered the pleas of the elders to marry and bear an heir. They steadfastly remained apart.

These tragedies went beyond the personal; in another place, another time, the consequences would be theirs alone. But here, those decisions blossomed into a communal sorrow. For centuries the Cochini Jews remained segregated, in the synagogue and marital bed. Neighbor against neighbor. Black against White. Exclusive in worship and love. If they had married one another earlier, if the elders had sanctioned love across the boundary, could this have saved them? These are the realities of Jew Town's star-crossed inheritors.

Living alongside them, celebrating Sabbath and holy festivals with them, witnessing their tears after burying Shalom, the brief burst of joy at a wedding feast for relatives overseas, I wanted to render up an account of a people who will soon be consigned to the archives, filed alongside other lost societies who failed to heed the siren of collapse.

As suffocating as the draining humidity of these coastal plains is the mood of a people afflicted by some kind of collective malaise, a brooding fatalism born of the realization that they are the architects of their own downfall. For some of them, the time of the Kerala Jews is already over. All that remains is to endure these final years as a spectacle for tourists in retribution for past sins of discrimination and discord. Privately, they mused, was it their curse or karma?

"We're not a *dying* community. The joke is, we're *already* dead," Gamy Salem observed from the parlor of his house on Synagogue Lane as he distractedly sipped masala chai in his parlor. "See how the tourists stare at us, like animals in the zoo, like the living relics we've become. Buy your two-rupee ticket, come see the Jew show while it lasts. This is our ending after two thousand years."

* * * *

THE LAST JEWS
OF KERALA

CHAPTER ONE

The White Jews of Synagogue Lane

"This land itself was a secret, shared between the sea and mountains, an illegitimate child of the two natural forces, protected by and provided for in a special way. Therefore, there was an assurance of plenty and peace."

—M.G.S. NARAYAN, *CULTURAL SYMBIOSIS IN KERALA*

K.J. Joy sat on the steps of the Paradesi Synagogue in Mattancherry and with the gesture of an open palm offered me a seat beside him. If ever a man lived up to his name, it was the *shamash* or caretaker of the local synagogue. In his fifties, he possessed still-boyish features and an equanimity that absorbed life's petty trials with easy humor. He was tall, with a languid air and a face of delicately wrought dark features lit by a smile that eclipsed the gloom around us.

He drew his knees up beneath his chin and clasped his arms around his legs in weariness. It had been a long day. Since early morning he had stood on sentry duty outside the sixteenth-century synagogue, shooing away the streams of tourists who came calling daily. Now as the sun melted into the ragged Mattancherry skyline and the evening settled around our shoulders like a blue-grey shroud, Mr. Joy could loosen the tensions of duty and relax.

It was October 1: Yom Kippur, Day of Atonement and fasting for the Jewish community. The synagogue doors were bolted and the houses of Synagogue Lane, home to the remaining handful of White Jews, were closed to the outside world. Doors and lower windows were shuttered tight, lace curtains on the upper windows drawn, lights off. The heat of the day yielded to a cool stillness, and an uneasy quiet pervaded. With the approach of nightfall, Synagogue Lane had become a place of repose for phantasmal shadows.

Mr. Joy cast a pensive glance down the one way street that is Synagogue Lane and the heart of Jew Town. Once a bustling community, it was now home to only twelve White Jews.

He had worked as caretaker at the synagogue for twenty-five years, taking responsibility for its daily upkeep, lighting the oil lamps for Shabbat and the festivals, polishing brass work, dusting chandeliers, chaperoning the hordes who came calling every day, corralling groups of excited school kids, explaining the history and generally keeping the public at bay and out of the path of the prickly Paradesi elders. Through it all, he remained composed, serene, sometimes a smile of mischievous amusement playing beneath his black moustache.

I pulled out my notebook containing a list of names, the names of the Cochini White Jews I had carefully gleaned from historical accounts and memoirs like jewels from the dust, and began to read them to Joy, who adopted the furtive manner of a Cold War spy betraying classified information to the enemy. His dark eyes darted towards the windows and doorways of the Jewish houses down the length of the street as he answered in a conspiratorial whisper:

"Dead. Dead. This one is also no more."

"What about him?" I asked, pointing out another name. He nodded in affirmation but then his voice dropped again in apology.

"*Alive*, but gone to Israel."

His finger continued down the page, as the roll-call of the dead grew longer until virtually all the names were crossed out and I had begun to wonder if anyone lived.

"Of course, this one stayed," he said happily, glad to offer some better news at last.

"Yes?" I said, brightening.

"But he died last year. This next fellow—dead. Here, Madamji, also expired, I'm afraid."

The list of "Ds" to denote the deceased carried on down the page and overleaf. I started again with a fresh piece of paper, this time writing down a sorrowfully brief cast of those who lived. I showed it to him to confirm.

"Correct. This list is living. But then, I tell you, they're old and they're sick," he added as if to caution against too much optimism. It was my first encounter with the community and already their fortunes seemed inauspicious.

"This is worse than I thought, Mr. Joy. Who can I talk to?"

"Talk? This is not a good time to talk, Madam," he explained, head wobbling in mild reproach. "You've come at the worst possible time. Why, only two weeks ago they buried another of their number. The last of the Cohen men. Shalom Cohen, brother of Sarah, was buried in this cemetery." He pointed into the distance of Jew Town, which lay ahead. "Since then, their mood has turned black. After the death of Shalom, they are just twelve. Imagine: to be old, to be the last of your kind, to *know* your time has come."

* * * *

Cochin lies on the Malabar coast of Kerala, a bounteous state on southern India's western seaboard. Through the ages it has been the scene of commercial trade and shipping and its cultural fusion of Indian, English, Dutch, Portuguese and even Chinese influences is a testament to a turbulent history of invasion first by traders, then foreign conquerors who battled to control this crucial Eastern spice route.

It was spices, as well as more exotic bounty such as peacocks and apes, that drew King Solomon's merchant seamen to these shores almost three thousand years ago. The connection with Israel and the Jews continued and after the fall of Jerusalem in 70 CE, Kerala was one of the natural safe havens that the Israelites turned to in their renewed period of banishment and persecution.

Their first major settlement was in the ancient trading port of Cranganore, also known as Shingly, which lies twenty kilometers north of modern day Cochin. But a series of natural and man-made disasters drove the Jews from their first established kingdom in India and they eventually resettled in Cochin from the fourteenth century onwards.

Kerala is flanked to the east by the densely forested mountains of the Western Ghats, the second highest range in India, which rises to more than 7,000 feet, and to the west is the Arabian Sea, the ancient seafaring highway for colonizers and traders. Along this fertile coastal strip, merchants came to buy commodities that are still grown for export to this day. It is said these lands once lay underwater until a major seismic force or volcanic eruption elevated the coastal planes to create a utopian landscape.

Today, Cochin is not a single place but a district, a cluster of lagoons, islands and inlets which are divided by narrow green waterways. Limpid, swamp-like waters crisscross low-lying islands, which are connected to the main bustling town of Ernakulam by bridges as well as ferries that act as taxis to and from the mainland. In the post-monsoon blossoming, flowers erupt in bursts of color from bushes and trees that overhang the network of backwaters. The dull expanse of water that separates the mainland from the islands is briefly transformed by a thick carpet of pink lotus flowers, as if the gods had cast confetti from the heavens.

Nature's miracle combination of low-lands and a profusion of water have created a lush, tropical beltway that yields abundant harvests of co-conuts, rice, exotic fruit, spices and seafood—all of which are packaged and sold throughout India and to markets beyond. Huge container ships from Europe and the Middle East dock in these islands, loading up export goods. Cochin is also a major manufacturer of coir matting and palm oil, which are predominantly for the domestic market. At dusk, the truck depot comes alive with activity and hollering as battalions of wiry-limbed workers load up huge drums of oil and bundles of coir beneath flood lights before dispatching into the night juddering convoys of gaily painted Tata trucks bearing the motoring legend "Horn Please!"

The Malabar coastline has long been a thriving commercial center. It was in this place that the first merchant Jews made their permanent home. The Black Jews, those of darker complexion who have a history that is said to date back to Solomon and a mixed ethnic lineage after intermarrying with the Indians, are settled on the mainland of Ernakulam. The White Jews, of more recent ancestry mostly dating to the early sixteenth century and hailing from Europe, eventually settled in Mattancherry.

The White Jews were traditionally landowners, businessmen or traders in muslin and perfume via Calcutta, as well as experts at cask-making and bookbinding, a skill for which they were renowned. In his 1861 memoir, *British and Native Cochin*, Charles Allen Lawson enthused: "with the most rude tools, they do certainly bind in a style far better adapted to the climate than any one of the brilliantly decorated exteriors of the London publications."

The Black Jews were also merchant traders as well as artisans: masons, sawyers and carpenters. Among both communities there were a few well off individuals who acted as money lenders, but by the early nineteenth century as Cochin declined as a result of Bombay and Calcutta usurping its position as the preeminent trading port, most of the Jews of Kerala had sunken into miserable poverty. Today there is little to indicate the glories of the past, when Malabar fuelled the ambitions of discoverers like Vasco da Gama and furnished the coffers of European kings.

Mattancherry itself lies just a couple of kilometers from the old historic quarter of Fort Cochin, which today is little more than a fishing harbor, marked by rows of Chinese-style fishing nets that are traced to the time of traders from the court of Kublai Khan. At high tide, the circular nets are lowered into the water by a winch system operated by three or four operators. The water's surface gives no hint of the fishy treasures that lie beneath. Each day when the nets are raised, a babble of excitement ripples through the harbor as the fishermen reveal glittering hauls of silver sardines, pomfret and grey shrimp as finely translucent as the skin of an old lady's fingers.

Wiry fishermen lever the nets out of the water and retrieve the cargo, which is then dispatched around the region in narrow rowboats that take the fish to market. Local stallholders buy the best of the stock fresh off the quayside and within minutes freshly fried fish, sometimes plain, sometimes with *masala*, is served up in newspaper cones to locals and tourists gathered around the local bars and taverns. At nighttime, when the stands do brisk business, the smell of fried fish is carried along for a good couple of kilometers if the wind is good. Strings of colored fairy lights give the dockside a festive atmosphere in the evening, a place to sit, gossip, sip cold beer and sniff the salt of Cochin's waterfront. Entertainment is provided by the promenade of rich sunburned tourists and elegant Malayalam ladies sashaying in jewel-like *saris* behind beer-barrel husbands, long white cotton *lunghis* tightly lashed beneath their paunches and stubby fingers carefully brushing their moustaches as they survey the local scene.

Makeshift stalls constructed of bamboo and plaited palm leaves sell tourist trifles such as polished conch shells, hippy beads, and tie-dye sarongs to flushed Westerners grappling with fists full of rupees. Hawkers sit on stools beside piles of freshly plucked tender green coconuts. Brandishing cut-throat sharp machetes, the coconut *wallahs* hack off the heads of the nuts to reveal a sliver of white flesh inside that holds the pale milky water. Children sit on the curb side, tiny hands grasping bulbous coconuts in their laps as they suck the milk through a straw, kohl-rimmed eyes gleaming with delight.

Walk through the streets and one will see a jumble of architectural styles, from the grand Dutch-style villas surrounded by high-walled rose gardens to a Portuguese-built basilica and the old St. Francis Church, which once held the remains of the explorer Vasco da Gama, who died in Cochin in 1524.

But Cochin is not just a resting place for the relics of old conquerors. It is a living testament to India's ability to endure its turbulent past and absorb it into the fabric of a pluralistic society. Here one can listen to the sound of church bell peels and the haunting cry of the muezzin overlaid with the sonorous lament of the conch shell blown by the high priest at the Hindu temple. Kerala remains a testament to India's religious co-existence, to its traditional ethos of tolerance, despite the periodic eruption of religious extremism that scars India's long history. It is here in Cochin that the Keralites have shown that Hindu and Christian, Muslim and Jew can retain a distinct religious identity and yet live in harmony. The Jews enjoyed a harmony that is rare in their history, living in peaceable accord with neighbors of every faith. It only served to sharpen the irony of their position further—the only discord they experienced was from within, the worst discrimination and humiliation they endured was at the hands of their fellow Jews.

With these thoughts, I approached Mattancherry's Jew Town the day after Yom Kippur, stopping at the top of Synagogue Lane. Today the street had sprung into life again as the local tourist shops got ready for the stream of visitors. In the distance, I could see one or two of the Paradesi or White Jews, dressed in the traditional Malayalam dress of cotton *lunghi*, yet distinctive by their pallor.

I looked up at the row of plastered stone houses, Jewish homes, many now empty or rented by the Kashmiri or Christian traders. Examining the otherwise simple, rather austere architecture, the eye was drawn to the intricate metal grillwork that covered the upper-story windows of the first few houses. On one house, the window grills portrayed the Star of David, painted in the same cornflower blue as the Israeli flag, the same resplendent blue of brilliant summer skies over Jerusalem. On the very next house was the ancient Sanskrit symbol of the Swastika, the Hindu symbol of well-being for thousands of years before it was hijacked and adulterated by the Nazis. On a third house was the crescent moon of Islam, picked out in green and white.

A Star of David, a Swastika and a Crescent of Islam all residing on Synagogue Lane. With a charge of excitement, I headed into the heart of Kerala's last White Jews towards the old synagogue.

* * * *

The Paradesi Synagogue sits at the very top of the one-way street that is Synagogue Lane, next to the local police station and a bookshop run by a Christian family. It is a simple, whitewashed rectangular building, with an attached clock tower that has four faces: one face inscribed with an in-scription in Hebrew, another in Malayalam and a third in English.

It was built in 1568 by the leaders from the White Jewish community known as the Paradesis, the Malayalam word for "foreigners", which refers to a group of wealthy European Jews who fled the Inquisition in Europe to settle in India and rebuild their lives. Some of these European Jews, es-caping persecution from countries like Spain and Portugal, intermarried with the older Jewish communities that had already been long settled in the region and came to Cochin from Cranganore after the great flood of the River Periyar in 1341 silted up the harbor there. But the majority of the Pa-radesis remained distinct, marrying within their community.

The Paradesi Synagogue is not the first to have been built in Ker-ala—there are synagogues with far older foundations—nor is it the most beautiful. But certainly, it is the most famous and it remains the oldest working synagogue in India. It is the only synagogue of the Cochini Jews that still holds religious services, albeit rarely, and it undoubtedly has a charm that casts its spell on all who visit.

It is this synagogue more than any other that put the Kerala Jews on the map, not just in India but worldwide, a cross between a museum and place of pilgrimage. Non-Jews come to learn of the amazing history. Jews come to pay tribute to one of the oldest of the Jewish Diaspora communities that is claimed by some to trace its lineage back to the ten Lost Tribes of Israel.

Inside, a young woman with curly short hair and huge dark eyes engulfing a thin sallow face sat at a wooden table with a small metal cash box set before her, alongside a notebook and pen. She was in her mid-thirties, yet her expression was weary, as if the burdens of an empire were bearing down upon her spare frame. And in some ways they were.

Her name was Yaheh Hallegua, daughter of Johnny and Juliette Hallegua, the sister of Sammy the synagogue warden. She had the familiar look of the Synagogue Lane women: wan complexion, long drawn out features, fleshy lips and a high forehead. Yaheh held a special place in the community: she was the only woman of marriageable and child-bearing age. The only bachelors were her cousins Keith and his brother Len. For more than a decade the elders had tried to force her to marry and bear a child to continue the Paradesi line. By refusing, she extinguished the dream of a reprieve.

Yaheh now spent her days at the synagogue selling tickets to visitors for two rupees a time, periodically shrilling instructions at them to cover their bare shoulders, or brusquely turning away those who disrespectfully wore above-the-knee skirts or shorts. She burned on a short fuse, seemingly bored and hugely irritated by the absence of variety in her years of responsibility as mistress of the gate, in charge of the endless cavalcade of tourists who all asked the same things and wore the same inappropriate dress. She retreated from the tedium by closing herself off to all around her, like a house with its shutters bolted tight to hide all signs of light and life inside. The grinding repetition of life in a one-way street was only part of her story. I was to learn later of her warmth and enjoy a smile that was as spectacular as it was unexpected. However, on that first day the expression was sour, the tone taciturn, the conversation cold to the point of inflicting verbal frostbite and it was with great relief that I saw Joy standing in the small courtyard outside the main synagogue itself. Mr. Sunshine was giving the tourists the synagogue spiel, telling the story with the contagious enthusiasm of a father reading bedtime stories to his children. I slipped off my shoes and went in to join him.

The old synagogue is typical of the Jewish Cochini style: rectangular in shape, with a narrow staircase to the right of the entrance leading to an upper gallery where the women once sat in *purdah* behind latticework screens. At the front of the central hall is the Ark, a wooden box or cupboard that houses the seven copies of the sacred Torah scrolls, hidden from view behind a silk hanging. Each of the ancient scrolls is contained within a cylindrical wooden casket that is covered with sheets of beaten silver, and atop each casket is a solid gold crown, studded with rubies, sapphires and emeralds, including one Torah crown donated by the Maharajah of Cochin in 1803. In front of the Ark is the *tevah*, a reading lectern on a small platform from which the Torah is read during services. Narrow wooden benches are arranged in a horseshoe shape around the edge of the synagogue, flanking the Ark on three sides. Light floods in from huge open-shuttered windows and broad dust-filled sunbeams crisscross the blue and white tiled floor.

The cool plastered walls are festooned with a rainbow of silk wall hangings: red, orange, purple, blue and shimmering gold that reflect the daylight. From the whitewashed, wooden-beamed ceiling hangs a glimmering myriad of Venetian and Belgian crystal chandeliers and lanterns: a mismatch of different sizes, shapes and colors that lend an air of baroque opulence to this otherwise modest structure. These days the lamps are rarely lit to display their full glory, for coconut oil to light the lanterns is expensive, and who would be there to see it apart from a handful of old timers? But on special occasions, such as the festival of Shimni, it remains the special duty of Mr. Joy to light the lanterns, to restore the synagogue to its full majesty. On these rare occasions, with diligent reverence the old Roman Catholic caretaker would mount his wooden stepladder and each chandelier would be carefully lowered, its crystal drops meticulously dusted, compartments filled with sweet-smelling coconut oil and then lit with a taper before being hoisted back into place. The most important lamp of all and the only one kept burning at all times is the *ner tamid* or "eternal light", suspended by a chain from the ceiling directly in front of the Ark. Those privileged enough to witness the Paradesi Synagogue in its fully lit splendor can never dispel the vision: one of ethereal brilliance, as if a tiny corner of heaven had fallen to earth for those few hours.

The floor of the synagogue is paved with hand-painted Chinese willow pattern tiles which were brought to Cochin in 1762. The tiles, each one bearing a unique design, were originally destined for the Hindu temple of the maharajah, but there are various legends about how the tiles ended up adorning the Paradesi synagogue. Gathering his audience around, Mr. Joy crouched low on the ground, fingertips splayed like a black starfish on the cool tiled floor as he gazed up at the circle of faces with shining eyes. Clearly the story of how the Jews secured the precious tiles was one of his favorites.

"See, how the story of these tiles tells of the cunning of the Paradesi Jews," he began. "One of the Jewish leaders saw the tiles that had been ordered by the raja. These were special tiles, each one different, each telling a new story, each hand-painted and sent in a special royal shipment from China. This one clever Jew saw the beauty of the tiles and wanted them for his synagogue. But how to persuade the raja not to use them in his temple? This was the problem. So, he told the king that the tiles were made using an ingredient that included the blood of a cow." He chuckled in delight at the audaciousness of such a scheme.

The story is recounted in the memoirs of Shlomo Reinman from Galicia, who came to Cochin and settled there in the 1840s after marrying a local Jewess. His writings tell of the king's horrified reaction when informed that tiles purchased for his sacred temple might be polluted with the blood of the sacred cow. "To think that he should tread upon a floor in which the blood of the cow he worshipped was killed and then mixed," said Shlomo's account. The tiles were duly rejected and given away to the neighboring synagogue for its own use, and to this day they remain one of the most remarkable features of the building.

Down the ages, the Jews gathered eye-catching treasures from around the world to furnish their beloved place of worship: chandeliers from Venice, tiles from China, sumptuous silks from Benares and a carpet from the former Ethiopian President Haile Selassie. The "Haile Selassie Carpet", as it is known, is unrolled before the Ark on only the most auspicious occasions. It was a gift from the man known as the Lion of Judah when he visited the synagogue during his period of rule, causing a security fracas at the time. When delivered to the synagogue, local police chiefs feared the rolled up carpet harbored hidden explosives and insisted on their men supervising the unpacking and unfurling of the carpet before clearing it for use.

The Lion of Judah is one of the many great and the good who came to pay tribute to this modest synagogue. To this day, generous visiting benefactors, both Jewish and non-Jewish, give donations to the synagogue to help finance its upkeep. It could scarcely survive without their charity or the patronage of the powerful. Its visitors' book includes the signatures of giants of history including Jawarhalal Nehru, Indira Gandhi, Lord Mountbatten and the Dalai Lama, among others.

And it has always been so. The White Jews were always a magnet for important visitors to Kerala. Even before the age of mass communication, their story fired the souls of intellectuals, travelers and the faithful who came to see this anthropological curiosity: a Jewish community who were as white as they were Indian. There are numerous historic chronicles on what they looked like, how they lived and indeed the feud that existed with their Black brethren across the waters. All outsiders noted the clear distinction that existed between the White and the Black Jews of Cochin, but because of their unusual appearance and their facility with European languages, the focus was always on the White Jews. Lawson gives an eye-witness account in his memoirs:

"The Cochin Jews are divided into two distinct classes, one known as the . . . White, the other as the Black Jews. The former are the descendants of the first settlers by marriage *solely* with one another. Their complexion is not exactly European, but it is the pale olive freshness most allied to it and the delicate carnation of the tips of the fingers proves that no native blood flows in their veins. The features are fine if not noble; broad and high forehead, roman nose, thick lips, generally concealed by a most luxuriant, jet-black curly beard."

His description of the women was less flattering and somewhat lacking in chivalry: "Whilst the Jew seems to improve in appearance as years creep on, the Jewess 'fades as the leaf fades', and at thirty years of age is plainness itself." The children were described as "leprously white".

Other accounts show how visitors were intrigued by this insular people, an alien culture who appeared to have dropped from the sky into the backwaters of India: "Jews, nothing but Jews, a pallid Jewry whose blood has been impoverished by the stifling houses and the Indian climate contrary to all recognized theory," writes Pierre Loti in his 1903 travelogue "India".

He adds: ". . . two thousand years of residence in Malabar have not in any way modified (the) Jewish faces. They are the same people, dressed in the same long robes that one meets at Jerusalem or at Tiberius; young women with delicate features, old wretches with hooked noses, children with pink and white complexions who wear paper curls over each ear just as their brothers do in Canaan."

Then as now, visitors were drawn to Synagogue Lane to marvel at the survival of this foreign clan, fascinated by their ability to survive in

India alongside the locals, thrive even with the establishment of their own businesses, whilst retaining an unmistakable purity of lineage. Yet there was something else that was sensed by one commentator after another: a faintly perceptible fatalism that ran through the Paradesis like intricate veins of black through white marble.

Even in the accounts of travelers from past centuries, there was recognition of a foreboding that prevailed over Jew Town. It was a jarring juxtaposition to discover in the midst of paradise, as Loti noted: "The decaying sadness and walled in isolation of this town seemed to assort ill with its setting of sky and palms, after taking this sudden turning one is no longer in India and the mind becomes bewildered, and we no longer know where we are; perhaps in the corner of a Leyden or Amsterdam ghetto that has been transported to a land whose tropical sun has baked and cleft its walls."

The writer rightfully placed the architecture of Synagogue Lane as Dutch-style: tall, tightly packed terraced stone houses with narrow windows that were not well suited to the stifling climate of Kerala's tropical climate. Reading his journal, it seemed that Loti felt almost claustrophobic by the insularity of life in Jew Town. They were in the heart of India, integrated and respected even, yet on another deeper level the Jews remained apart, distinct, a refugee people. For the Jews, Kerala was always meant to be no more than an interim homeland, a sanctuary until they could return to the land of their forefathers, ending their spiritual dislocation.

In the past a yearning for their homeland may have been the cause of the Jews' melancholy. But by the new millennium, many of them had returned home, to Israel, leaving the few who remained to languish in a new sadness: ironically, a realization that soon their community would be lost to India forever.

Among the twelve Jews that remained on Synagogue Lane, the First Couple of Mattencherry's White Jews was the synagogue warden Sammy and his wife Queenie, daughter of the late Sattu Koder, wealthy businessman and Jewish patriarch. Their children had left long ago for America and the couple now lived alone in a grand house, cared for by a devoted retinue of servants. A few doors down lived Johnny and his wife Juliette. Johnny also helped run the synagogue, dealing with its upkeep and administration, and his younger daughter Yaheh lived with them. Yaheh's beautiful older sister had left long ago to marry and settle in Israel, where she lived with her husband and three children. "All boys," her mother joyfully told me.

Blossom Hallegua lived towards the top end of the lane with her sons Keith and Len. Blossom was now in poor health, bedridden and reliant upon her sons for survival. Blossom's boys were the last eligible "young men" left in Synagogue Lane, in their late thirties and forties, and both had resisted efforts to marry. Keith had once been a promising local businessman, running his own travel firm, which catered to tourists, but since coming into family money he had retreated more and more from public view and now he was a virtual recluse. During my entire stay I never saw him or his brother once and locals living on the street told me that Keith had become a changed man in recent years, preferring to lock himself away for days on end. He never came to synagogue, he never went to parties much and he rarely went out. "There was a time when we used to sit, gossip, he was fun. But lately, he's not been . . . the same. There's something that's not quite right," said one of his neighbors, *sotto voce*.

Isaac Ashkenazy was another bachelor, although advanced in years and now in his ninth decade. But unlike the Byronesque brooding of his younger neighbors, Isaac was joyful in his solitude. He had never married, resisting all efforts with a violent passion, and he continued to live alone in the old family house called Sassoon Hall. He was an elusive figure, of thoughtful disposition and dressed in immaculate white *kurta pyjama*. Isaac was the image of Alfred Hitchcock and in true Hitchcock style would make dramatic yet fleeting appearances when least expected, head turning slightly to fix his audience with large, baleful eyes for just a split second before slipping into the shadows of his grand mansion. There was no point knocking on the door, tapping at windows, telephoning even: he refused to be drawn out. When we finally did get round to meeting at a party he turned out to be adorable company: sweet, funny and with a rather giddy sense of humor, giggling like a saucy schoolboy about the need to avoid marriage and predatory women at all costs. "Especially at my age," as he put it.

Isaac's neighbor was Sarah Cohen and her neighbors on the other side were the Salems. Gamy Salem was a Black Jew who had married Reema, a Paradesi. They were Jew Town's only "mixed" couple.

This was the last twelve, a number that included Gamy, who was as dark skinned as they come but had honorary "White" status through marriage. I was yet to meet the Ernakulam or Black Jews across the waters, a community that had a completely different dynamic: younger, more integrated and, curiously happier and more reconciled to their shared fate of extinction.

How was it that this became their shared destiny? There was no plague on their houses, no war, nor famine to drive them into the abyss. Theirs had been a comfortable co-existence with their countrymen. While other Diaspora communities had thrived through adversity, the Cochini Jews had embraced demise in an earthly paradise. In the end, death came not at the hands of others, but one another.

The question was why? The elders, keepers of history, were as good a place as any to start looking for the answer.

* * * *

CHAPTER TWO

King of the Indian Jews

"I traveled from Spain.
I heard of the city of Shingly.
I longed to see an Israeli King.
Him, I saw with my own eyes."

—RABBI NISSIM, FOURTEENTH-CENTURY POET AND TRAVELER

Within days of my arrival, I had become a stalker of the Jews of Synagogue Lane. I invaded their "natural habitat," lurking amidst the camouflage of the Kashmiri shops while I scanned the horizon for their distinctive markings: white skin and silver heads encased in *kippah* caps. Once I spotted my prey, the quiet thrill of adrenalin coursed through my body as I homed in silently, mercilessly, until I was there, upon their very necks.

I targeted the biggest beast in the forest first: synagogue warden Sammy, the man with all the answers, I was told. It proved to be a risky endeavor as I would be the one who eventually received a mauling from the aged community patriarch.

Sammy was an elusive and mercurial character. Some spoke of him as a prickly yet kindly old buffer who came from one of the oldest and grandest of families of White Jews, who had married the richest Jewess in town, thereby cementing his position in the pantheon of elders. His detractors castigated a proud and arrogant man, prone to outbursts of anger, one privately tormented by the realization that the Paradesi Synagogue would be closed at the end of his lifetime, on his watch. Sammy lived with the knowledge that he would go down in history as the last warden of the last working synagogue in Kerala. His was the inevitable legacy of failure.

He was not the easiest man to like. But it was easier to understand the source of his volatile moods. Every time a stranger visited, every time he explained the story of his people, an unspoken question hung in the air: why did it end? Behind the glittering façade of success, beyond the decorous glory of the synagogue and the history that stretched behind them like a golden-paved pathway leading to their Jerusalem, there was the realization that the road lying ahead was a wasteland stripped of the hope that only youth can bring to an exhausted generation. For the Jews of Cochin, the future could promise only endings.

The others had the luxury of hiding behind their lace-draped shutters, screening out reality if they wished, but Sammy was the man in the public eye who dealt with that question every day.

The pressure upon him was particularly keen at this time of year, which was at the height of the festival season. I had landed on the day of Yom Kippur, the day of abstinence and reconciliation which had seen this small community pray and fast for almost twenty-four hours. The timing was not deliberate, yet it proved far from ideal as the community was stretched—emotionally and physically. Despite most of the community being in their seventies or eighties, they had prayed inside the synagogue for hours on end, much of it standing, after taking no food or water from daybreak to sundown.

As I waited outside his house, chatting to the Kashmiri family who ran the emporium opposite the Hallegua home, word had reached the warden that a stranger was in town who was asking questions about the history of the Jews of Cochin.

A servant emerged from the Hallegua house and crossed the lane to speak to me: "The Master wishes to know what you want." As I explained, he listened avidly, head wobbling from side to side in careful appreciation and then scuttled through the brown shuttered doors to report back. At the upstairs windows of the Hallegua house, the curtains fluttered and one could discern the shadow of someone looking out onto the street. I sat on a stool and waited, my only source of amusement being the ambling promenade of tourists who ran the gauntlet of the Kashmiri merchants.

A while later he emerged, a gaunt figure in white *kurta pyjama*, accompanied by his wife, Queenie, who followed behind. Queenie lived up to her aristocratic reputation, blessed with an imperial bearing and melodramatic glamour that seemed out of place amidst the provincial goings-on of Cochin. Like a Picasso masterpiece-made-flesh, she made her way toward the car, her mouth a gash of lipstick red across a white, meticulously powdered face, her hair carefully coiffed into a halo of curls around a domed forehead. The two were on their way to a shopping expedition and their driver was polishing down the white Ambassador car in anticipation of their departure. He then stood to attention by the backseat door, holding it open for them. With a look of regal curiosity, as if examining a new species of insect under a microscope, Queenie gave me the once over before sweeping into the back of the car, uttering not a word.

An audience of local Keralites and Kashmiris had gathered by now to witness the encounter with Sammy, who came over to speak with me. His face was a mask of small, hard features, with any emotion disguised beneath a veneer of hauteur. His light eyes were clouded over with milky cataracts, his mouth a tight little line, complexion blanched under the pitiless light of the noon sun and the only discernible color in his face was the bulbous blue veins prominent at his temples. I extended my hand and took his in mine: his palm felt dry and papery, with neither warmth nor welcome in its touch.

"You're seeking information on the Jews of Cochin," he said, aware of the people gathered around us, keen to play to the gallery. "What do you wish to know?"

"I'm looking for some guidance on the history."

"I've no time for guidance. Every day we're besieged by people like you: journalists, writers, tourists. They come knowing nothing, nothing of our history, thinking I've the time to do nothing but talk."

"I know you're a busy man. So, I've come prepared . . ." I began, feeling less like the predator and more like a child protesting to the headmaster.

"Then write your list of questions, leave them at my house and I'll make an appointment for you Wednesday or Thursday, before the festivals begin again."

There were no pleasantries, no chit-chat. With that he was off, stooping to join his wife in the backseat before being driven into town, the wheels of the Ambassador leaving the rest of us engulfed in a puff of dust as the car peeled off. It was a cold little introduction, but it was a start.

The gathered audience of Kashmiri storekeepers, servants and hangers-on broke into animated conversation, congratulating me on crossing the first hurdle. "Now all you have to do is get him to keep his promise," added one. "Maybe he will, or maybe he won't." A few doors down I could see Gamy Salem standing at his doorway, hand jauntily propped up against the shutters as he looked on with a wry little smile. Something about that smile set off an alarm bell in my head.

That same day I dropped off my list of questions with my local residence details attached. The servant opened the door of the Hallegua residence and accepted the piece of paper with lowered eyes and open palms, as if receiving an ambassadorial missive. "Thanking you, Madam. The Master shall see it."

Days passed. Tuesday came. Wednesday came, then Thursday. Tomorrow would be Friday, the beginning of a period of festivals which would go on for a couple of weeks. The Sabbath deadline was looming, so with rising anxiety, I paid another visit to the warden's house. I was in luck. Sammy was conversing with one of the neighbors outside his home. He finished up his conversation and approached with a spark of malevolent delight in his eyes.

"Your questions are no good," he announced in a booming voice that ensured everyone heard. "I don't have time to answer your questions." Was this a genuine "no" or the usual Indian prelude to negotiations? I cast my mind back to my list. But the warden was unmoved and raised the temperature of our exchange.

"The answers are obvious. You've chosen to ask questions about the history of the Black and White Jews. We don't wish to discuss the past. *That* history is finished."

"Perhaps it'd be helpful to hear your side of the story."

"*We* are the first. What else to say? I don't care what the history books claim. I've no time for questions. I've no time for interviews."

"What about next week. Anytime," I responded. "I've come especially from London to meet you."

"Then you've wasted your journey, Madam."

A look of triumph flitted across his face as he shoved the piece of paper back into my hands, turned and went into his house. Through all this exchange, Gamy was standing on his threshold overlooking the scene, his face a picture of wry amusement still, as if to say "I could have told you this was coming."

The exchange had been the nearest thing to drama that Jew Town had seen in weeks. It was amusing viewing: the foreigner spending her days stalking the cantankerous Paradesi warden, day in, day out. Who would break first? After watching in silence, the traders and hangers-on broke into renewed chatter, a cacophony of Malayalam, Kashmiri and Hindi as they gathered around in a conspiratorial huddle, hands gesticulating as if swatting flies above their heads as they expressed particular outrage that I should be addressed so brusquely while several months pregnant.

"Sit down, come into the shade, take water. To speak to a pregnant woman like this! They say he's arrogant and now you see it yourself," said one of the shopkeepers, offering me a stool next to a basket of bronze Ganeshes, the Hindu god for removal of obstacles. The Kashmiri, ever the wily salesman, quietly suggested the purchase of a Ganesh might prove fortuitous.

"*Now* you're seeing the nature of this man. This isn't the first time, I'm telling you," added another. "Arre, Gamy. Tell her."

Gamy wobbled his head, a typically ambivalent Indian gesture for tricky situations that could be taken any number of ways: yes, no, possibly, or no comment. I showed Gamy my list of questions. He sucked his long yellowed teeth and then with great deliberation untied and retied his *lunghi* extra tight beneath his small round stomach, as if preparing to deliver a devastating verdict.

"See. This question here," he pointed halfway down the page. "You mention innocently, 'What is the historical relationship between the Black and White Jews'. Then you mention in passing the great ancestor of the Cochini Jews, Joseph Rabban," said Gamy, head now bobbling excitedly as he tapped away at the list.

"See. The problem is not that you know too *little* of our history. The problem is you know too *much*. Our Sammy doesn't want people to know the truth. That the White Jews persecuted the Blacks. That there was apartheid. That the great forefather Joseph Rabban was a Black Jew, not a White. If you had come knowing nothing, you'd have your interview by now. You'd be welcomed with open arms. Then Sammy could tell it the way he wanted. He *knows* you know the real story. *That* Madam, is your problem."

According to Gamy, Sammy was not just the warden but the keeper of its legacy, charged with preserving what remained: a wonderful story of endurance. As I sat sweating amid the raffia baskets, the pregnancy hormones were raging. I decided I would bide my time, calm myself and then return to the synagogue the next day to try again. Surely even the notorious Sammy Hallegua could not say no to a pregnant woman inside the synagogue just hours before the Sabbath?

The next day at the synagogue, I readied myself to meet Sammy on his own territory. It was approaching eleven o'clock and already the humidity had left man and beast listless. The neighborhood crows hunched in the trees in a sun-drunken stupor like intoxicated sleepy old men about to keel from their branches. The street was quiet. Most of the residents were holed up inside, legs aloft on their planters' chairs as they sipped *nimbu panni* and iced *lassi* beneath softly whirring ceiling fans. Cotton bed sheets hung from the open doorways to block out the fierce light, periodically catching a breath of breeze and fluttering up towards the sky like white-gloved hands waving their goodbyes. The Kashmiris, used to the pine-cool climes of the Himalayas, were the only ones who stood by their trading posts, wilting by the roadside as they lifted rose-water-soaked handkerchiefs to cool their brows. In the local police station next door to the synagogue, the sole sign of life was the khaki-clad duty officer spread-eagled in a chair near the door, *danda* skew-whiff as he snored in happy oblivion with a litter of pups fast asleep at his feet.

As I entered the synagogue antechamber, Yaheh avoided eye contact as I paid my two rupees to get in. Clearly, the word on the street was that Sammy had no intention of helping, and I feared the community would now close ranks on me before I had even started. Unbowed, I slipped off my shoes and went into the main chamber.

The synagogue was empty save for Joy doing some light dusting, and Sammy, holding court with a couple of foreign tourists clad in short pants, t-shirts and wraparound sunglasses. He was a different man from the one I'd met earlier: his eyes were animated and his countenance bright. He was regaling his audience with the story of how the White Jews were the original settlers in Cochin. I joined the group and listened in.

"Are there any books for sale?" asked one man with an American accent, reaching for the wallet in his back pocket.

"There're no books, I'm afraid. But you can buy postcards just outside," Sammy replied amiably.

As the Americans prepared to leave, again I broached the subject of speaking with Sammy. But the impending Sabbath had not induced a new mood of benevolence, after all. Sammy exploded in fury. His face turned puce and his arms flailed to the rafters like the tentacles of a disturbed squid.

"We have no need for any book on our history," he screamed. "We had two professors live with us for one year. We helped them, we told them the truth and what did they write? Errors and lies."

"What lies?"

"I have no time for you people. You can go to hell," he said, and began to walk away.

"I don't give a *damn*," he yelled. "This is *my* synagogue. *Mine*. And I will do what I wish with it. I can close the doors to all visitors. I can ban everyone if this is my wish and they can go to hell if they don't like it."

He stormed out of the building in great sweeping strides, leaving us to digest the outburst in a silence only broken by the mocking chirruping of the parakeet outside. Within the hour, word had spread through the street about how Sammy had raged at a pregnant woman inside the synagogue. The neighboring bookseller, Godfrey, had told the neighboring Kashmiri shopkeeper, who told the antiques emporium manager who told the next store and the next, until the story was passed on to the other Jews living on the street. Only the sleeping policeman missed out on the drama. My worry now was that the White Jews would freeze me out, following the example of their leader. Instead, as news of the synagogue standoff spread, strangely, it brought out the best in the Paradesis. Even

Isaac Ashkenazy, the resident Hitchcock look-alike, paused to give a fleeting glance of sorrowful condolence before vanishing once more like a zephyr into the shadows. As I walked past the Kashmiri shops, the stall-holders paused to commiserate. "Don't mind," said one. "He's like this. Sometimes he just goes crazy."

As I passed Gamy Salem's house, the old cynic stood watching by his doorway. The wry smile of amusement had vanished, replaced by a look of mild concern. He called me over and ushered me into his parlor with the offer of a glass of Mirinda fizzy orange. It was the best offer I'd had since my arrival. After days of being stonewalled, finally there was a breach in the Paradesi defenses. Ironically, the breach had been made by the warden himself.

"Sit. Drink," instructed Gamy as his diminutive servant Mary laid out refreshments on paper napkins by way of reparation. "What you need to know? I've got five minutes."

* * * *

What was this history, one that Sammy was so keen to bury? The White Jews, save for Gamy who was really a Black who married one of the "others", fell silent when asked about the past. Yet the problem between the Black and the White Jews was central to understanding why the Cochin Jews had come to such a premature end.

Gamy and Reema were the exception, not the rule, and their mixed marriage was accepted only now, when the end was in sight. But for centuries marriage between the Blacks and the Whites had been taboo. The two communities were distinct and the Blacks were effectively barred from the Whites' synagogue. That more than anything rankled still.

At the heart of the division was the argument over who came first, who were the *real* Jews of Cochin? While Sammy offered a sanitized account of the past, for the Black Jews of Ernakulam the shadows of past grievances merely lengthened with the passage of time.

Sammy may not have wanted to disclose *his* version of that history, but it was laid out for all to see in a series of simple mural paintings in the antechamber of the Paradesi Synagogue. A series of pictures with brief captions beneath told the Paradesis' official story: that they were the ones that hailed back to the days of Solomon, that they were the first to land in Kerala, that their ancestor was the reputed elder and founding father Joseph Rabban. There was no mention of another community of Black Jews across the water in Ernakulam. Each year streams of visitors from around the world came to see the Paradesi Synagogue and its murals. As far as those visitors were concerned, this was the whole truth.

Central to the identity and mythology of the Kerala Jews—whether Black or White—is a place called Cranganore, also known as Shingly. Just as Jerusalem lies at the core of Jewish identity, so Cranganore is at the core of the Cochini Jewish identity.

The ruler was the so-called King of Shingly, Joseph Rabban, an elder who was welcomed like a raja by the people of Kerala when he first arrived. He has an almost mythological place in the heart of the community and its history, not unlike that of King David in Jerusalem.

The two cities are twinned in the historical narrative of Cochini Jews. Jerusalem was sacked, leading to the dispersal of the Jews in 70 CE.

So, a natural disaster and war drove out the Kerala Jews from that first kingdom, leading them to resettle in Cochin. The pain of exile from Jerusalem is matched by a second from Cranganore, that first settlement. To this day, the Cochini Jews will not visit Cranganore unless absolutely necessary and if they have no choice then they are careful to ensure they leave before sunset, fearing disaster will befall them if they remain when darkness sets in. Cranganore remains a name synonymous with tragedy, a place where the twin specters of death and banishment still linger. Yet in recognition of its symbolic importance to the Jews, every one of the community is still buried with a handful of earth from their old settlement, in memory of those first settlers.

This symbolism meant that just as the Cochini Jews were keen to prove they hailed from Israel, so they were also keen to prove they came from the line of the first Jews to settle at Cranganore. Such lineage conferred status, a purity of heritage. Purity of heritage was also hugely important in Hinduism, and those who were seen as the oldest and purest among the Jews were accorded greatest respect by the Brahmin classes of Kerala. More importantly, in Hindu India, status translated into economic and political power. For these reasons, the need to prove a link with Jerusalem and Cranganore was vital.

In the account *A Jewish King at Shingly*, authors Nathan Katz and Ellen Goldberg wrote about the "symbolic intertwining of Jerusalem and Cranganore." They also noted "there was a sibling-like rivalry between the Paradesi and Malabari Jews over who were the rightful heirs of the line of Joseph Rabban" and his ancient kingdom. The Malabari Jews were another name for the Black community of Ernakulam and its nearby villages.

But who was Joseph Rabban? Centuries after he landed on Kerala's shores, he remains the man who in many ways personifies Cochini Jewish identity, and his legacy is the subject of this tug of war. Inside the Paradesi Synagogue antechamber, Rabban features center stage in the paintings that depict the "history" of the Jews of Cochin. This is the version that the White Jews choose to give to the outside world, a blend of fact as well as myth.

The early paintings show Shingly, as it is known in Malayalam or by its Anglo-Indian name of Cranganore. The first connection is established by a mural that depicts a teeming bazaar. The caption reads: "There was trade between King Solomon's Palestine and the Malabar Coast." That much is fact.

The next painting shows the destruction of the Second Temple after which the Jews of the holy city scattered to all the compass points. The third painting shows a ship settling on a lush coastline. "Landing of the Jews at Shingly," reads the legend beneath. Thus, the first proper Jewish settlement was established in India.

The series then leaps several centuries forward to a seminal moment—the arrival of the legendary patriarch. An Indian king greets a shipload of Jewish migrants on their arrival in Kerala, bedecked in as lavish a finery as a maharajah could muster, with full entourage bearing colored parasols and beating drums. "The Raja of Cranganore receives the Jews," declares the solemn caption.

The leader of the Jews is then portrayed in the audience chamber of the raja's palace, receiving a gift from the kingdom. This marks the real arrival of the Jews in Cochini society, no longer just another class of immigrant trading serfs, but now a favored people in their adoptive land, a chosen few, no less.

Little of the Cochini Jews' history is documented, but the story of their special status under the raja is recorded by one key artifact: a set of copper plates engraved with a royal decree. Cochini tradition says the plates were awarded to Joseph Rabban in 379 CE and they represent the clearest evidence of the antiquity of this community. The Paradesi elders says the original plates are kept in the Ark inside their synagogue, but scholars differ in opinion on the antiquity of these particular copper plates, with some dating them as late as 1000 CE.

The plates state that the Hindu king of Malabar awarded Rabban the village of Anjuvannam and its revenues as well as according him the right to certain privileges of the ruling class, such as riding an elephant, being carried aloft on a palanquin and being shielded by his very own state parasol! The three small rectangular copper plates are engraved in an ancient Tamil language written in the Vetteluttu script. A translation reads:

> "Hail and Prosperity. The following gift was graciously made by him who had assumed the title King of Kings. His majesty the King Shri Parkaran Iravi Vanmar whose ancestors have been wielding the scepter for many hundred thousand years ... was pleased to make the following gifts: We have granted Joseph Rabban the village of Anjuvannam together with propriety rights, tolls on boats and carts, the revenue and the title of Anjuvannam, the lamp of the day, cloth spread in front to walk on a palanquin, a parasol, a Vaduga drum, trumpet, a gateway, a garland, decoration with festoons and so forth. We have granted him the land tax and the weight tax; moreover we have

sanctioned with these copper plates that he need not pay the dues which the inhabitants of the other cities pay the Royal Palace and that he may enjoy the benefits they enjoy."

The gift of Anjuvannam is made in perpetuity to Rabban's successors or as the charter poetically phrases it: "so long as the world and moon exist".

The Jews' charter was unique in that it granted them rights that were usually the preserve of the royal family alone, including firing three salutes at daybreak and on the day of a marriage. Naturally, both sides of the Cochini Jewish family wanted to claim Rabban as their own, thereby eulogizing him in word and song. He who hailed from Joseph Rabban hailed from a line of kings.

In the Malayalam folksongs, recorded by the women of the community in handwritten notebooks and handed down the generations, there is a wedding song that likens Joseph Rabban to a handsome bridegroom. These songs are a musical history of the people, so it is unsurprising that Joseph Rabban, their idealized first man, should feature so prominently. The lyric of one wedding song said on the day of marriage "the bridegroom is like Joseph Rabban, he is like a king."

To the Jews of Kerala, Joseph Rabban was everything: founding father. Groom to the bride, Cochin's Jewish people. And King of the Jews in this realm of the East.

A link back to this Jewish King of Shingly was proof of purity. The White Jews insisted that they were the true ancestors of this line and I guessed that in a way Sammy saw himself as the natural inheritor of Joseph Rabban himself. Any questioning of this truth, the truth of the

Parsadesi Jews, was a questioning of the position of Sammy Hallegua himself, as well as his ancestors.

But there was a second, even more controversial test of Jewish status for the Paradesi community: color. The white skinned Jews claimed their very pallor was proof of their purity.

Their people had predominantly hailed from Europe: many of their number arrived in India after fleeing religious persecution during the Inquisition of the sixteenth century. On reaching the Malabar coastline they found another older community of Jews, but one which was darker skinned and fully integrated with the local Cochini people. Some of those European Jews married some of the Jews who originated from Cranganore. But there was evidence of tensions creeping between the Black and White communities early on. David Mandelbaum, an academic who studied the Cochini Jewry extensively in the twentieth century, wrote of how the European Jews on their arrival in India found it difficult to relate to their brethren, who differed in so many ways.

Keen to distinguish themselves, the Paradesis claimed they had never been polluted by non-Jewish blood. They claimed to have a deeper understanding of the Torah and Jewish knowledge and sought to distance themselves in order to win a higher place in the caste-based society of Cochin. Just as the higher caste members of the Kerala Hindu society segregated themselves from others on the basis of religious purity, so the Paradesis distanced themselves from the Malabari Jews.

It marked the beginning of a new era of division within the Cochini Jewish family. The Paradesis claimed they were the oldest line of Jews in Cochin—even though many of them hailed from Europe during the Inquisition period and there was evidence that the Malabar Jews were indeed older. The Paradesis were equally quick to insist that they had the purest Jewish blood, evident by their white skin. Their facility with European languages and trade links with the West positioned them well with the royal court, allowing them to easily propagate their version of history not just to the local dignitaries but also to influential visitors. They began to spread the story that the Black Jews, already well established in the region, were not "pure" but the descendants of slaves who had come on the ships of Solomon and then married local Cochini women, thereby polluting the Jewish maternal bloodline.

The taint of slavery in caste-based Kerala proved devastating and would lead to the decline of the Malabaris in Cochini society. Claims that the Malabaris were somehow lesser Jews naturally outraged the people of Ernakulam and its surrounding villages, who claim they are descended from what was known as the old "southside" synagogue that once existed in Cranganore. They found their beloved ancestral figure Joseph Rabban had been hijacked by the newcomers. To this day the Black Jews claim the copper plates housed in the Paradesi Synagogue were stolen from them way back in their history, although they have no proof of this. More fundamentally, the Blacks found themselves usurped in their own historical narrative—a story that went back to Joseph Rabban and his fateful meeting with the raja in Cranganore, then back further still to the days of King Solomon. The Malabaris believed it was *they* who hailed from kings. The holy cities of Jerusalem and Cranganore were their inheritance and the betrayal by the Paradesi Jews had now placed all this under threat.

So the battlelines were drawn, coursing through the brackish green waters that separated Mattancherry and Ernakulam. As the Whites fought ruthlessly for preeminence in Cochini society, the scene was set for the introduction of a policy of color separation, a Jewish apartheid in India that would last for centuries and eventually lead to the decline and fall of both Black and White.

* * * *

CHAPTER THREE

The End of Shalom

"May all blessings be upon you;
May you be blessed with children and shalom.
Be blessed and multiply in the earth.
Take possession to divide it, so that you may survive."

—A COCHINI BLESSING FROM *JEWISH WOMEN'S SONGS FROM KERALA,*
AS SUNG BY SARAH COHEN AND RUBY HALLEGUA

S halom's funeral had sent ripples of foreboding through this tiny community, awakening the old dread, unsettling the mundane routines of life, its effect magnified because they were so few in number. Each family carried the burden in its own way, fiercely protective and guarded against outsiders who would prey upon their tragedy. Of the twelve White Jews who remained, the majority were in their late seventies or eighties, with only three "youngsters"—those in their late thirties and forties. There were no young newlyweds living on this street, no sulky teenagers consumed with their own selfish traumas, no rascal kids or chubby babies to elevate the elders from the mire of the past.

This was the strangest thing about life on Synagogue Lane: everyone seemed to be in countdown mode. The Jews themselves were counting the number of those still standing, taking mental bets on who might be next, while they counted down the diminishing days of their own existence. The Muslims and Christians on this street were counting their profits or potential profits to be made from this dying and world-famous community. Soon, Synagogue Lane would no longer be home to the White Jews, but an anthropological curiosity, with boarded houses up for grabs to be turned into souvenir shops or cafes for the tourists. The prey and the predator shared Synagogue Lane, their fortunes entwined.

When one spoke of the Kerala Jews, one inevitably reached for the epithet "last". The last young Jew, the last young Jewess, the last *shohet*, the last working synagogue, the last marriage and the last birth on the street, which was so long ago no one could rightly remember.

Sarah was the "last" of the Cohens, the family that drew its name from the priestly line of the *kohanim*. But it was even more basic than that, for she was the last of her household: first her parents, then her husband and now her brother had passed away. Hers had been a barren marriage, so the house was empty of heirs and now the subject of the cunning plotting of her servants and hangers-on who all wanted to wrest this pricey piece of real estate from her grasp.

Strangely enough, when I first arrived, no one wanted to talk to me *except* for Sarah. My thoughts seemed to resonate with hers, being of the end. Having Shalom taken from her so unexpectedly had brought to the surface reflections about what was left, for her, her people and how it had come to this point.

Sarah's house sits at the very top end of Synagogue Lane, near the first Kashmiri tourist shops. The windows of her house were protected with metal grills depicting the Star of David and painted in red, white and a sky blue. During the day the hallway of her house was converted into a shop selling embroidered goods.

She sat in a chair by the door in a small rectangle of yellow sunlight, her knees set apart, toes idly twiddling on the cool tiled floor. A copy of the Torah was open in her lap, its pages flapping in the breeze as she stared off into the distance. This was Sarah's favorite spot: sitting inside her doorway, looking out onto the street. It was a prime viewing position and from here Sarah knew she would miss nothing and hear everything. From here she would note the caravan of tourists and passersby on their way to the synagogue at the top of the lane, straining to catch stray gossip like a child netting butterflies.

The shutter doors of her house were open, leading into a long narrow corridor, a darkened haven from the white heat. Inside were tables and rails laden with folded piles of embroidered Jewish *kippahs*, white silk tableware for special festivals, embroidered with golden and silver thread. At the back of her store was the more workaday stock, damask and linen tablecloths and napkin sets, embroidered with pink rosebuds and bordered in lace, gingham cotton dresses for small children, with frills and flounces in keeping with flamboyant southern Indian tastes. These and other goods were sold to tourists to bring in a little income now that she had no means of support.

I had seen and heard about Sarah from books, pictures and stories about the community. Being the oldest surviving lady, she was the grand dame of Cochini White Jewry. Her husband had been Jacob or "Dickie" Cohen, from one of the less well off Paradesi families and a lawyer by training. A community leader, Dickie had been one of the few qualified under Jewish law to teach the younger boys about the faith. He died long ago, taking that tradition with him to the grave. The couple had been at the core of this community back then, a kind of Posh Spice and David Beckham of Cochin: the "it" couple who led the prayers and the partying, the drinking and joking that used to be part and parcel of Cochin Jewish life.

Today, I found an old woman who was a faded facsimile of that past life, a worn out spirit engulfed by grief. Shalom was given the full traditional burial rites accorded to a member of the white Jewish community. Sarah described the traditions, sometimes slipping into generic descriptions of a Cochini funeral to lessen the pain of returning to that day in September 2006. His body was buried in their special graveyard just a few hundred meters away—a graveyard that once had forbidden the burial of their so-called "Black Jewish" brethren alongside the Whites.

Despite being in mourning, Sarah seemed to welcome company, crave it even, and invited me to pull up a chair and share her ringside view. As a young woman, she had been a vivacious creature, with a lusty gap-toothed smile that had captivated Dickie all those years ago. I got the sense that theirs had been a passionate relationship. She was a young woman barely into her twenties, he a middle aged man who fell for the kid next door with the sexy figure and head of wild black curls. Sarah had never been a beauty, but had an earthy quality that enabled her to ensnare one of Jew Town's most eligible men.

The fierce midday sunlight was a harsh judge as it fell upon her face, making her squint irritably. Her long countenance was lengthened further by crepe-like folds of skin that hung from her jaw-line, her mouth and eyes etched with deep lines that told stories of tremendous happiness as well as pain. Her skin remained a creamy luminescent white despite the intense Kerala heat. She retained her trademark wiry curls, now steel grey instead of black. Grief and time had played mischief with her health and looks, drawing black rings around drooping eyes which had sunken into hollows.

She was dressed in white, wearing a sleeveless top that exposed fleshy batwing arms and a striped cotton sarong that was tied about her waist. She cradled her right hand in her lap, keen to draw attention to it. A week ago, in careless distraction she had splashed boiling tea on herself, taking off the skin on the back of the hand, leaving it red-raw, with ragged brown edges fraying around the wound.

"I must not touch it," she told me, touching it, "or it will bleed." She bit her bottom lip and then with a sucking motion, she moved her dentures in and out of their sockets, looking at me with big mournful eyes.

She asked what I was doing in Cochin and as I explained she said the Jews were in the midst of the most important series of autumn festivals. So again, my timing was not fortuitous. I had been warned even before I came that the community was notoriously closed to the point of outright hostility.

But luckily for me, Sarah wanted to talk. Her conversation was candid, irreverent and invariably indiscreet. She told me it was time the story was told. There was no point delaying as these were the last days and one had to get the story on paper while there were still those left alive to tell it. Already she feared they had become no more than living museum pieces. Every day streams of tourists, Jew and non-Jew, Indian and foreign, paraded this street in gawping huddles, clad in the ubiquitous uniform of vest, hiking shorts and rucksack. One could see the Jews twitching with irritation from behind their lace curtains as they surveyed this defilement of their community. The tourists knew no bounds, poking their heads inside the doorways of the Jews' houses, scrutinizing the latest exhibit before moving on. Some came in genuine tribute, armed with information about the Jews' migration to these shores and a fascination with their lasting endurance in India. Others were simply on the Lonely Planet tourist trail. After Synagogue Lane came the local shops, an *ayurvedic* massage and then lunch at the nearby coffee shop where Brad Pitt once hung out to drink *lassi*.

In the old days, the whole town had been theirs—the Jews. No strangers came walking down *their* street, into *their* synagogue, let alone their homes. Or if they did, the occurrence was rare and sanctioned. Today tourism had almost become a *raison d'etre*, with the synagogue already accorded future museum status by the Archeological Survey of India.

"This was once our place, full of only our people," said Sarah. "Now after the others left, gone to Israel, gone overseas, or just gone—the Kashmiris, the Muslims, the Christians have come. They're good people, they take care of us. But they're not our kind. The old life is gone. Where is it now? *Nothing*."

"What was it like, when you, Dickie and Shalom lived here, when it was all Jewish?"

"On festival nights we'd sing, we'd visit each other's houses, food would be prepared and shared. The men would drink, tell jokes and old stories. The woman would sing Cochini wedding songs, cook together for the festivals, play cards on tables set out in the street. Now, hardly ever do we sit out. And there's nobody to talk to. If there's a party, who'll come? The old, the dead?"

Losing Shalom was losing the remaining part of the life shared by her, her brother and her beloved Dickie. Shalom had been the older brother, but more than that, he was a companion and friend. He was the firstborn to the Cohen family in Jew Town, a well-to-do and educated family in the Paradesi community.

There were four children in the family: first Shalom, then Sarah, then another sister and then a brother whose birth coincided with tragedy. All four kids were born in the house of Queenie, who came from a high Jewish family that held vast estates of land and property portfolios and had business interests across the region. When she married Sammy the two Paradesi dynasties and their riches were united.

After Sarah's youngest sibling was born in Queenie's house, on the day of the baby's circumcision, the mother was taken ill. "In the evening my mother came home from the synagogue and began violently purging. The doctor was called and he gave her medicine but it didn't stop. After endless days of purging she died, leaving four small children."

Stricken with grief, the father took Shalom to Bombay to live and left the youngest children, including Sarah, to be brought up by their grandparents on Synagogue Lane. So she lost both parents in short succession. Her father remarried and Shalom grew up in Bombay and worked for the family's printing press. Business was good and the family's fortunes prospered, but her elder brother and father had become strangers.

With her male guardians far from home as she grew up, Sarah turned into a willful young woman. In her twenties she caused a minor scandal when she defied her father by marrying her next door neighbor Dickie Cohen. It was his second marriage and some of the neighbors suggested in hushed tones that their love pre-dated the death of Dickie's first and much older wife. But Sarah remained unapologetic.

"I was in love. We lived in the same town, on the same street; we saw each other every day. We fell in love. It was like that. Father didn't like, so he came and took me to Bombay."

Dickie was not the kind of man who gave up. He pursued Sarah to Bombay where she lived the dull life of the dutiful daughter, imprisoned in the confines meted out by her father. He rescued her from her concrete tower-block and the couple escaped into the pulsating thrills of the metropolis where they married in secret and in reckless defiance of her father's wishes. They returned to Jew Town as man and wife and set up home, their love an open challenge to the elders. Here was a young man, who on paper seemed the perfect suitor. Why had her father been so opposed?

"This was Dickie's second marriage. In a way, that was nothing important: he was a Jew, he was a lawyer, and he was a Cohen. There was nothing wrong with him, that I shouldn't marry him. He was also very good looking. He followed me to Bombay, we got married. Finished."

Their love was exclusive and remained so, until Shalom joined their household years later after the death of his father. He never married and so moved in with Sarah and her husband. By then the rest of the family had left, so the three lived happily under the same roof for their remaining years. When Dickie passed away, the bond between brother and sister grew stronger. Shalom and Sarah had become companions, friends and confidantes. So when Shalom suffered his accident a few months earlier and was plunged into a coma from which he never recovered, the impact on Sarah was devastating, bringing her blue sky crashing down upon her head.

We could hear the bolt straining against her main door. The rain had started to pour down, coming down in gusting sheets that caused rivulets of dark water to swell and overflow from the guttering, rushing down the street. The pungent smell of damp earth rose from outside and entered through the open windows, engulfing the house with a sweet muskiness. The guests at the door were the night watchman and one of the old servants from the town—both Christians. They had come for their regular evening's viewing of the Malayalam soap opera that began at 7:30 PM. The three, including Sarah, would normally settle down in the living room in front of the TV each night and together they passed time—she sharing her relative wealth with them, regardless of religion and caste. In the past, the White Jews attached great importance to such things as status and their in-bred superiority, but an increased vulnerability had made for greater accommodation.

The two settled down in the other room: the old woman in a white *sari* neatly folded her skinny limbs into the windowsill like a rag doll, the watchman perched on a chair in the corner directly opposite the TV, a bag of gram nuts in his lap and legs akimbo, as they absorbed themselves with the latest dramatized epic on the Hindu god Lord Krishna. Sarah and I returned to the back room, with the sound of the ululating Malayalam drama pulsating through the house like a crazy heartbeat.

The rain drummed relentlessly outside, adding its backbeat to the symphony of theater coming from the television set. Sarah resumed her place at the table and piled more food onto my plate. The simple act of serving me had triggered memories of mealtimes with her brother. In memory of lost loved ones, it is said that the Jews will sometimes set places for the dead at table.

"I really miss him most now," she told me, "at the time of my food." Her voice cracked, as she wiped tears from her eyes and then blew her nose into the tea towel. She looked at the place opposite where he used to sit. "When we used to sit here, when I'd eat especially, I always liked to push the dishes to him. 'Shalom. Eat,' I'd tell him." She pushed imaginary plates in my direction.

"I liked to watch him taste the dishes I'd prepared, I liked to watch him eat until he become full. I'd tell him when the synagogue services were happening, when there were festival prayers, who was visiting, who was leaving. In the evening, I'd tell him when Johnny and Sammy had gone to the synagogue and say 'Shalom, dress up and come.'"

"Did he like the synagogue?"

"He'd always wear his best suit to go to there. Always, the best suit." She paused to blow her nose.

He sounded like a fine man, I said in a hollow voice, feeling with each passing moment like a vulture feasting on the sorrows of strangers.

"He *was* a fine man," she continued, her spaniel eyes lighting up for the first time since we'd met. "A quiet fellow. He never used to fight with anybody. When anybody came he would talk. He got on with anyone. That was Shalom's way."

Without prompting she recounted the night of the accident; words, details, feelings, pieces of a nightmare that cascaded from her memory out into the open, until that evening was laid bare before us as clearly as a series of Polaroid photographs lying scattered on the table: "It was just another night, we had dinner, we talked, we went upstairs. As usual, I went off to bed. After an hour or so I saw Shalom hasn't come back from the toilet, so I thought maybe he's purging or he wet his pants. I got up.

'Shalom is not here, Shalom has not come,' I tell myself." Her eyes were now looking beyond me, beyond this room.

The architecture of the row of Jewish houses on Synagogue Lane is unusual, with a linking corridor or room on the upper floor, allowing families from one house to come into the neighboring home if needed. That night in a panic, Sarah called out to Gamy's wife, Reema, who lived next door.

"I thought he must be in the toilet, but the door wasn't closed. Shalom wasn't there. Luckily, Reema was awake at 10:30 PM. I called out. She said to go down and open the door and see where he'd gone. I went down the stairs, just two steps and there, at the foot of the stairs, I saw Shalom on the floor in a pool of blood. His head was cut from here to here," she indicated with her right hand a huge gaping gash across his skull.

"He had no sickness, nothing to complain of. No asthma, no pressure. Nothing. He was that healthy. Then this! Straight away I took him to the hospital."

Shalom was in a deep coma. Two months after the fall his condition deteriorated and he died. It was a stupid accident and a pointless death. As a member of the Paradesi Jews, he was accorded full funeral rites lasting several days and buried in the cemetery reserved for the White Jews. Sammy, the synagogue warden, and his brother Johnny led the duties on the men's side. Sarah fulfilled her duty to buy the white material that was stitched into a shroud. "I took my machine into the synagogue to stitch it. The men of the synagogue had the duty of giving the last bath to Shalom's body, a purification rite. In this way, we pulled together."

Shalom's abrupt departure underlined the frailty of those left. Many had died in recent years and many more had migrated. The result was a street where the houses were empty, or with one or two people living where once there had been whole extended families. His death was the final in a series of losses for Sarah, which began decades ago with the breaking up of her community following the creation of Israel.

"It began thirty, forty years ago. When the Cochini Jews decided to pack up and go, they sold their houses—to pay for the travel to Israel. One by one we watched the houses sell up. As a girl, the noise on this street was incredible. We were such a loud community, too much noise, I'd say. We were never scared. *Now* we're scared."

It seemed such a strange choice of word. Why scared, I asked.

"Because we feel lonely. A terrible loneliness, to lose your people, to know the end is coming. Our neighbors, the Muslims, the Kashmiris are good friends to us, but there's nobody here when they close their shops at night. They close and go home. Nobody among them lives here, not a single person.

"These last few years have seen too much stress. Too much is sitting on our heads. It's *we* who must bury our last friends, close our synagogue forever one day soon, watch our houses sold to speculators. This is why sometimes Sammy and the others get angry. Angry at outsiders who come to watch us die. Angry at those who abandoned us."

"You blame those who left?" I asked, skipping over the fact that I was here for just that—to witness their demise.

"What can we feel?" she murmured softly, the trace of betrayal in her voice. "They're determined to go, they'll go. Let them go. We remain here. Finished."

"If life was so good for the Jews, Sarah, why did so many leave? You seemed to have it all."

"It's true, we *were* happy, very happy," she agreed, sucking her dentures in contemplation. She used her tongue to push the lower palate out of its socket so that it protruded from her lips before snapping it back into place. "But, see, those who passed out from college, they found no jobs here. Abroad they'll get a job. Some went to Israel, some went from Israel to America. And the young ones, where were the partners? Husbands, wives? For these reasons, they had to go."

There were still a few youngsters left, both Black and White Jews, so why didn't they come together and marry to allow the old Cochini line to continue? It was a loaded question, as I knew the old resentment still festered. The Paradesi Jews were afraid of how history would judge their treatment of the fellow Jews across the water: outcast from their synagogue because of color, an act that went against the essence of Judaism, the sense of justice that was the source of *shalom*. Sarah summed up the dirty past succinctly.

"The Whites stuck to our own. The Blacks, the same. Besides what young people do we have here? We've just one or two and they can't stand one another. If we force the topic of marriage, they go *wild*. We cannot force them. We've given up."

"So, this is it," I said, all of a sudden infected by the pessimism around me, the oppressive drumming of the rain overhead, not to mention the prospect of spending my evening with one Jewish and two Christian pensioners watching a Hindu religious epic in Malayalam. "After all that has happened, millennia of history, from Solomon's Israel to twenty-first century India, it will end. Just like that."

"What are you talking?" she said irritably, as she reached for another *pakora*, crumbs scattering from her lips like bitter words. "It is ended *already*. Even now we don't have enough men to hold Shabbat prayer. Without the people from Ernakulum, there'd be no prayers on festival. We can't eat meat unless their *shohet* cuts it first. *They* only are keeping us alive."

The White Jews of Synagogue Lane were on a life support mechanism, alive only because their old rivals were keeping them alive. The Paradesis had gone from living on the same street, eating from the same plate, sharing the same synagogue, in and out of one another's houses, being part of every development of one another's lives, from birth to *bar mitzvah*, from marriage to funeral, to this. Something beyond even death. The end of their history. The end of *shalom*.

* * * *

CHAPTER FOUR

The Gentle Executioner

"A man's table is like the altar."
—THE TALMUD

History has a habit of biting back. There was a time when the Paradesi Jews refused to eat kosher meat that was killed by a Black Jewish hand. The Paradesis had their own *shohet* and the Malabaris theirs. The meat cut by one side was not eaten by the other. When Dickie Cohen died, Synagogue Lane lost its *shohet* and the only kosher slaughterer who remained was Elias "Babu" Joseph, a Black Jew from Ernakulam. If the Paradesis wanted to eat meat then they had to take meat cut by Babu's hand. The irony was not lost on Babu, a man who felt keenly the injuries of the past.

Babu was the last *shohet* for the entire Cochini Jewry and after him there is nobody to take his place. I arranged to meet him at his place of business, Cochin Blossoms, just off Jew Street in Ernakulam, an aquarium and garden center housed in a disused synagogue. Jew Street was once the exclusive enclave of the local Jewish community and all the houses and local businesses were owned by their people. Today it is a religious mix, with just a handful of families remaining amidst Muslim,

Hindu and Christian alike. There are two synagogues on this road, one of which is still in rare use for special occasions once or twice a year, when visiting Jews help to make up the quorum for prayers. In contrast, a few doors down, tucked off a narrow alleyway is the local mosque, which is packed at prayer daily. Five times a day the cry of *namaaz* echoes through the old Jewish quarter.

Babu's shop was around the corner from Jew Street and set in the antechamber of Ernakulam's disused second synagogue. The synagogue was engulfed by the hullabaloo of the local bazaar, a mostly pedestrian zone where one can buy all manner of goods, from electrical items to copper-bottomed cooking pots, bolts of block-printed cotton to flutter-ing silk *kaftans*. The stores have names that befit the retailing buzz of a big town: "Kerala Fancy Goods", "The Lunghi Emporium" and "The Exclusive International Handbag Company" are just some of the hand-painted signs overhanging the dense thoroughfare populated by honk-ing *tongas,* rickshaws and pitiful mules, bent low beneath their parcels like put-upon husbands.

Set amidst the chaotic sprawl of stores, stalls and twisting alleys bris-tling with shoppers was the aquarium in the old Tekkumbagam syna-gogue. The narrow pathway to the synagogue was lined with potted plants, casting a dappled shadow overhead. The courtyard outside the large stone and timber structured building was neatly filled with row upon row of flowers, palms, creeping vines with white blossoms, seedlings of geranium, bougainvillea and herbs. Each plant was lovingly nourished with water and shielded from the harsh sunlight with a green netting canopy.

Up the stone steps and through huge wooden doors painted a dark brown, inside one discovered a shady haven filled with banks of fish tanks

that had an immediate calming effect. Babu's desk and chair were positioned exactly opposite the entrance, giving him a clear view of all visitors. The desk was spread with papers, brochures on the latest exotic fish,
fish husbandry, lists of local suppliers and so on. On top of his desk shelf
he had a row of glass pots filled with tight bundles of Chinese bamboo,
bound in red tinsel, for good luck and prosperity.

His aquarium empire lay behind: scores of tanks filled with bubbling
green water and fish: suspended myriads of color. Some were water-borne
jewels of bright red and yellow, the size of a finger nail. Others were
aquatic birds of paradise, with plume-like fins fanning out in shimmering display. The tanks were clean and well aerated and the fish looked
well cared for, loved even.

For clearly this was more than simply profit and loss. Babu gave his
fish life and in turn they bestowed a kind of peace. His prize specimen
was the endangered Arowana, the legendary dragon fish of Asia. The fish
is highly prized and auspicious, considered to be lucky in some countries.
It is a collector's piece. The full grown Arowana looked like a Supreme
Court judge, with its distinguished whiskers and jutting jaw as it paraded majestically up and down its own private super-size tank. In a
nearby smaller tank was a younger, green Arowana, a quarter of the size.
Despite its best efforts it lacked the majesty of the full grown version,
rather like a young man hopelessly trying to emulate his father by sport-
ing a downy moustache.

Railings were suspended from the ceiling, along with colored glass
lanterns. From the rails hung bunches of packets containing plastic
toys and plants to landscape the fish tanks. His employees, a bunch of
wiry-limbed Muslim boys, were unpacking boxes when I arrived. They

removed clear plastic bags filled with water and new stocks of fish. As they unloaded the bags, the shop floor was transformed into a surreal scene: aisles filled with scores of gently bobbling balloons of water, each cradling its own multi-colored shoal of exotic fish. The balloons gently lolled from side to side, bumping one another, like giant soap bubbles. One by one, the boys took the bags, popped them open and decanted the fish into a tank.

Seeing me arrive, Babu called on one of the many assistants to come and man the phones. He was a tall and strong-looking man, with kind brown eyes, dark polished skin and a thick neatly cut head of salt and pepper hair.

Babu was forty-nine years old and married to a Bene Israel Jewess called Ofra. They had two daughters aged eighteen and fifteen and the family was part of the twenty-two Jews that lived in Ernakulam. The Tekkumbagam Synagogue at the back of his aquarium and now in disuse was built in remembrance of the first synagogue in Cranganore, known as the "southside" synagogue because of its location on the river.

The synagogue itself could be reached by passing through the aquarium, through another set of doors at the back. The doorway was partially blocked by piles of sacks filled with fish feed and other supplies. But once inside the synagogue chamber, one was struck by its particular beauty, simpler, more austere and yet just as arresting as the synagogue in Mattancherry. The Tekkumbagam Synagogue has ten windows representing the commandments and two pillars which are meant to evoke the pillars at the entrance of the Temple of Solomon.

The place was in shadow as the shutters remained bolted. Instead of the smell of oil lamps and incense was the aroma of neglect, where there were once garlands of jasmine, cobwebs now dangled in silver tapestries from beams overhead. Only the antechamber lived on.

When this synagogue was still active, the Jewish children were taught Bible classes here. This particular community did not have rabbis, but scholars known as *hamim*. The Jewish children learned the Torah, as well as the old Shingly songs, poems and Hebrew. They came not just on Sabbath, but every day after school. The synagogue was the epicenter, the source of knowledge, meaning and life. As the Jewish community diminished over the years and the need for a place of worship became redundant, Babu took over and converted part of the building. In deference to its past, he did not touch the place of worship itself, merely converting the front part into his aquarium. Its Ark remained, but the copies of the Torah were removed and sent to Israel long ago. So, where Jewish children once sat cross-legged on the flag-stone floor to recite the Torah, their curled ringlets bobbing at their ears as they prayed, tanks of tropical fish now reside in desiccated splendor.

Babu grabbed a brown paper bag which he slipped into his trouser pocket and a blue *kippah* cap which was placed in the other. "Now, we must go," he said, striding towards the door. On the Thursday morning before the weekend of Simhat Torah, I joined the last remaining *shohet* in action at Cochini Market for the slaughter of the chickens.

Every few weeks or in the run-up to a major festival, the White Jews send an Ambassador taxi to Babu's aquarium, which is a forty-minute drive from Mattancherry. The taxi driver hands over a fold of rupee notes to pay for the chickens that Babu must purchase and then slaughter for the white community. In the run-up to Simhat Torah, one of the biggest celebrations of the year, each community was busy preparing for a lavish banquet. Babu was tasked with cutting the meat for the White Jews and sending it back in plastic bags on the backseat of the taxi.

It was just one example of how the Black and White Jews had become mutually dependant in their twilight years: forced to forgo the past and cooperate so a *minyan* of ten men may be formed in the Paradesi synagogue for special festivals, so they may eat meat at their now infrequent banquets, in rare communion for a few days of the year. The two communities reminded me of a quarrelling old couple, cherishing old grievances to their bosom, harking to past betrayals, yet sticking by one other in advanced age and adversity because there was no one else.

The Cochin market itself was a gourmand's paradise, with great sacks packed tight as drums with spices that tickled the senses: cardamom, *jeera*, turmeric, chilly powder, cloves, anise stars, cinnamon sticks. Also on sale were roughly broken pieces of the natural brown sweetener *jaggery*, used in cakes and desserts. Sesame seed-encrusted ladoos in trays and cling film, plastic bowls bobbing with saffron-drenched *rasmalai* and syrupy *gulab jamun*. Mounds of tender green coconuts, papaya, watermelon, bunches of tiny black seedless grapes and every type of banana imaginable—red, green, large extra gelatinous yellow and the tiny yellow finger sized bananas that are most prized. The eye was drawn to wicker baskets of green gooseberries the size of plums, bulbous and delicately veined, like plucked eyeballs. All manner of vegetable fuelled the appetite: tiny sweet potatoes little bigger than the tip of one's thumb, bundles of spinach and the bitter green *methi*, fragrant bouquets of *dhania* and mint, gleaming aubergine and cartloads of red onion, tomato and garlic, the staples of the Indian kitchen.

Pass through this section and one entered a large courtyard that was jostling with fishmongers and fisherwomen, squatting low on their haunches, skirts and *lunghis* hoisted above the knees as they sat over stone gullies which carried the blood and dirty water into the drains. The workers cleaned, gutted and stacked piles of glistening silver sardines, mullet and pomfret as well as rarer catch such as sea bass. Grey pyramids of fresh prawn and shrimp dried on newspapers alongside aluminum bowls of round clams the size of a penny coin and crabs that would fit in the small palm of a child. The cacophony of hollering fishwives bartering in Malayalam was deafening.

Beyond the fish section was the meat quarter, where hanks of mutton marbled with bright yellow fat hung from hooks over butcher counters, swinging pendulously in the shimmering heat. At the very back of this compound, up a flight of steps was the live chicken quarter—the smell of feathers and the butcher's block hit you before the sight of scores of wire and wooden chicken coops, packed to bursting point with white chickens. The coops were stacked in a square around a central workstation, a roughly hewn table of hardwood stained with dried blood. A pile of old giblets sat in one corner, waiting to be cleared away, providing a bloody feast for the fat black flies that swarmed busily.

There was an old fashioned set of scales to weigh the birds. The birds selected for the Jewish table must be of the same weight and size, without any physical defect or blemish. Even after slaughter if a bird is found to have some internal ailment, the entire carcass is jettisoned. Around thirty fowl had been selected and set aside in a separate pen. As I arrived, the dreadful lottery of death came to a close as the last few birds were selected and drawn in squawking dismay to be weighed.

Babu stepped up to the butcher's block. It was as if the chickens knew their executioner had arrived. He was silent, dignified, mentally preparing himself for the religious duty. He took out his blue cotton *kippah* and placed it on his head before carefully removing the special blade from its sheaf of brown paper and sharpening it slowly, one side, then the other, with great deliberation across a whetstone. He was assisted by one of the market men, who prepared a jug of water and stood opposite Babu. Two other boys, also non-Jewish, waited by the chopping counter, their hatchets ready to skin and carve up the birds once the kosher ceremony was completed.

Babu's assistant removed the first bird from the cage. Its terror was palpable, eyes bulging, wings flapping frantically. The screeching reverberated through the market as the other chickens watched in silence, heads cocked.

Babu began the Hebrew prayer that must precede the killing, praying for the life that God gave, the life he was about to take away. The assistant dipped the chicken's head into the jug of water, forcing it to take water and swallow. The reflex action brought the bird's main jugular vein into prominence in its neck, and as the assistant held the body and wings, Babu pulled the head towards him, stretching its neck out and securing the thick vein and cartilage between his finger and thumb. Silenced, the bird looked unblinkingly into Babu's eyes as gently yet firmly he sliced the bird's neck in three short cuts of the blade. It was over in less than a second and the chicken's limp body was laid on the chopping block, its soft white feathers drenched crimson with blood. One of the boys took the bird's carcass. It was defeathered, skinned and butchered into pieces within the minute.

Babu and his assistants continued the production line of slaughter until within thirty minutes all the fowl were killed and cut. During the entire process Babu's face remained a mask of impassivity and he spoke not a single word. After it was over, he took his blade, washed it down in a fresh jug of water and then poured the pink, blood-stained contents onto the stone floor. He wiped down the blade, removed the brown paper sheaf from his pocket and slid the blade back in. Then he washed and dried his hands, removed the *kippah*, folded it and placed it deep into his other trouser pocket. As he completed his ritual, Babu's gaze fell to the ground, drawn by tiny dark spots of blood that stared up at him like accusatory eyes of the dead.

* * * *

An hour later we were settled in chairs in the green coolness of the aquarium again. After leaving the meat district on our return, we had been waylaid in the fish section of the market as Babu's eye was caught by a spectacular seabass weighing in at six kilos and glisteningly fresh. The festival season was upon us and this weekend marked two of the most important dates in the Jewish calendar, Shmini and Simhat Torah, so Babu wanted to buy something special for dinner. He agreed a price of 1,050 rupees. The specimen, he pronounced, was perfect in age, weight and texture, as we watched it being wrapped up like fish groupies. "Such a fish doesn't come along every day," Babu explained with quiet excitement.

As soon as we settled at his office he made a flurry of calls to local families and had agreed to split the cost with them and share the delicacy out for the special festival dinner that lay ahead. Already, there was a sense of excitement building, akin to the run-up to Diwali or Christmas. It was a far cry from the White Jews of Synagogue Lane, enveloped in a fog of despondency, where the synagogue warden stomped the streets in ill temper and impatience. Sammy would also be hosting a party on Friday night to celebrate the beginning of the festival of Shmini. In attendance would be the great and good of Cochin, non-Jews. The other Jews on his street were invited for a drink, but many said they would not attend the dinner.

In the past, Sammy's late father in law, Sattu Koder, hosted parties for all the Jewish neighbors as well. The street was alive with celebrations or parties of one sort or another for days. When the old warden died, the effervescence of those nights was also extinguished and today each family preferred to return home for a special meal and raise a toast in their own house.

But the Ernakulam Jews still prayed together and partied together on all special occasions. This Friday night, after prayers, they planned to sit down at one table for dinner. It had been so in the past and it remained so still; hence, the air of expectation and Babu's delight in securing his seabass. As we discussed the preparations ahead, Babu visibly relaxed, eased into his chair and exuded an air of serenity that was much in keeping with the calmness of his garden and aquarium.

The conversation turned to whether the Black and White Jews would be celebrating together over the coming days and Babu explained that such unions were rare. The old insults still burned. As he sipped his chai, looking out over the garden, the softness in his eyes dissipated and was replaced by a fire I had not seen until now: "What bullshit, they talk," he murmured softly.

"*We* are the first Jews in Kerala. Our ancestors came from Cranganore, our history dates back to the beginning. I can show you a tombstone of one of our people that dates back to the thirteenth century. They freely admit their ancestors came from Europe only in the fifteenth century. So how can they be first?"

The tombstone he referred to was the oldest Jewish gravestone in Kerala. It was dated 1269 and found in the tiny Malabari village of Chennamangalam. There the Jews had once lived under the protection of a local chieftain called the Paliat Achan. The tombstone written in Hebrew stands outside the Chennamangalam Synagogue, which has been renovated and turned into a museum.

"If it's so evident," I asked, "why do many still believe they are the original Jews of Cochin?"

"Because people go to them, to the other Jew Town, they listen to one side of the story, a partial history and they believe the whites were the first and only Jews. They swallow this story. But it's bullshit. And I'm sorry for this language, but I've no other word," he said. "They choose not to recognize an older community just forty minutes away in Ernakulam. One that was larger than theirs and longer in tradition in Kerala. Instead, we're subjected to this humbug that they're the first and true Jews."

It was awkward, but I asked about the Paradesi claim that the Malabari Jews were descended from slaves. The question was like lighting the touch-paper on a Diwali firecracker.

"They call us sons of slaves. It makes me angry when they say this. Our ancestor was the great Joseph Rabban and, before that, the Jewish merchants who came to India after the fall of the Second Temple in Jerusalem. Our line goes back to the Holy City itself. They can only truly say for sure their line goes back to Spain. Yet, because they're rich, because they have the white skin, their story is more exotic, more romantic. It's swallowed whole, no questions."

Babu's blood pressure was up and he needed to take tea to calm down. An aquarium was a good place for him to be, a kind of occupational therapy. So much for the Paradesis' claim that the old Black-White tensions were over. Babu passed his hand over his moustaches, swiftly brushing them back and forth as he gathered his thoughts before lifting the glass to his lips. The chai did its work, slaking his thirst and soothing his anger.

"I was taught Hebrew by my father, you know. My mother, who's very orthodox, insisted. She was a tough lady. He taught me little, I admit, so I can't teach my own children. But it's the same with the White Jews, now they've no hereditary priest. They've no scholars. The last true scholar was Jacob Cohen.

"Now, he was a man of their community I admired. Jacob Cohen was a man with a sharp mind, a wonderful person, a genius, a great teacher. It was he who told me to learn to cut the chicken in the kosher way. He was the only man who could do so and he said to me 'One day I will die and go and who will cut the chicken for the Jews then? You must learn, you must carry on. I'll teach you.'

"For three years he taught me. I was in my mid thirties. Jacob was a man who could see far into the future, he could predict the problems. He blamed Koder, who was Queenie's father, and said because of him the community was dying. Koder was a rich man and he could have helped more people, then maybe more would have stayed and not gone to Israel.

"His daughter Queenie married her first cousin Sammy, from another wealthy family but nowhere like Koder's wealth. This is their way—to keep the skin pure but more important, to keep the money inside the family. This history of intermarriage, interbreeding, what has it led to? This refusal to marry Black Jews? It has led to death. To their diminishment, to a tiny group of people who are brilliant but without purpose, too eccentric or in some cases just mad. Many are unmarried, many are without children. How can such a community go on?"

Babu explained how most of the people on both sides of the water were poor. Not everyone had the riches of the Koders and Halleguas, or even the modest wealth of Babu. For these people, Israel represented not just a spiritual return, but a chance to build a new life.

"For them the State of Israel was a Promised Land in more than one way. It was a land of milk and honey. So they went for a better life. What to lose?"

Just as the youngsters had fled Mattancherry, Babu feared the last young Jews of Ernakulam would also be pulled away by the simple forces of economics—that and the lack of marriage partners.

"Of our twenty-two people, the youngest is my daughter who is fifteen," he said. "You know, we've five people under twenty years. About 60 percent are under forty years, the rest are old. That's not bad. But even for us, it is ending. The younger generation don't want to learn Torah and our boys rarely go to synagogue. Ours is a dispersed community now. In the past there was pressure to observe. People watched. 'Who's missing synagogue? Why?'"

Even in Babu's day, the choice of brides was limited and in the end he defied his "militant" mother by marrying a woman from the Bene

Israel Jews in Mumbai. As the father of two daughters, the headache is much worse now. But unlike his mother, Babu had no plans to bully his children to conform. "I see an even worse problem for my daughters," he said. "My elder daughter doesn't want to stay."

"What does she want to do?"

"Oh, she dreams of NASA, the space mission. She's brilliant at science: 99 percent for maths, 98 percent for physics, 97 percent for chemistry. She'll go if she gets the chance. The younger one is totally the opposite. She's relaxed. She doesn't worry about her future, a job, a husband. One wants to go to the very top, be the first. The second says 'Papa, I don't mind being last, as long as I am happy'," he laughed and patted his moustaches with evident pride at the thought of them both.

"But I wish for them a good husband, from good family, with good job. Such a man is more important than any Black or White Jewish thing. Now there're no Jews here for them to marry, so what to do? We have to look to the Jews elsewhere. Bring new blood back to Cochin.

"We have to make our choice. Or be like the others and simply die."

* * * *

The next day was the first night of Shmini, followed by Simhat Torah, when the community celebrated the end of the yearly cycle of reading their holy book. Also, falling on a Friday, it would coincide with preparations for Sabbath.

Babu asked me to join him and his wife for lunch on Friday, when she would also be making some preparations for that evening. Then in the evening I was asked to come to their prayer service at their other syna-

gogue in Ernakulam, Kadavunbagam, and join the celebratory meal afterwards. After the cold reception I had received from the senior-most elder
of the White Jews, Sammy, I was touched. It meant a lot and I accepted.

I arrived at Babu's home the next day at lunchtime. It was a small,
square, whitewashed house, with a gateway and path to the side leading
to the main entrance and hallway. The first door on the left opened into
a bedroom, followed by a second door that led into the living and dining
room. The kitchen was at the back of the house and was abuzz with activity, the heat of cooking steam and the clatter of pots and pans. A wonderful smell of curry and savories filled the entire house. The dining room
was painted a cool blue, with open windows on either side allowing a
pleasant cross-breeze.

I sat at the large dining table and was quickly given a glass of pulped
black grape juice by Ofra. She was a pretty woman in her forties, with
black hair tied into a bun, warm brown eyes and a rounded frame. Her
marriage to Babu had been a love match. Babu saw her at the synagogue
in Bombay and was taken immediately.

She was a diligent wife and mother, rising every day at five for
prayers and then preparing the children's breakfasts and meals and packing the youngest one off to preschool tuition by six thirty. The oldest one
was studying at college some three hours distance away and came back
at weekends to see the family. Ofra's duties also involved assisting the
Ernakulam Jewish community in things like preparation of food for the
festival season and keeping an eye on those who may need extra help.

That morning was particularly frantic and she looked exhausted, but
her activity was undiminished. Her forehead shone with sweat and her
forearms were damp with the exertion of beating the sundown deadline.

Ofra and the servant were busy preparing snacks for the post-prayer dinner at the synagogue, the three meals for Sabbath and the Simhat Torah festival which would be shared with the Muslim servants, plus lunch for all of us today. The young Muslim assistants from the aquarium had popped by as Babu told them to get their lunch at his house that day. The teenaged boys leaned against the wall, drinking juice as they joked and chatted with the lady of the house while waiting for their meal. The mood was light and affectionate and they seemed more like her sons than her husband's employees; there was nothing to indicate that one was Jew and the others Muslim. Everyone was caught up in the festival bonhomie.

The Sabbath meals were hot and ready in great aluminium cooking pots. As the servants prepared to leave, she hunched over the pots and ladled portions into tiffin cans for them to carry home to their families. "Since it's festival, we share our food with them," she explained to me. "It's something we like to do. For many years we couldn't afford it because of the children, but now they're older we like to do this again," she said. The dishes were a red chilly chicken curry, *pilau* and vegetable dish.

Having fed the boys, she turned her attention to making pastries to take to the party that evening. The main food would be catered by the daughter of the most senior elder among the Black Jews, Isaac Joshua. But Ofra had offered to at least provide some of the snacks.

She stood at the dining table, chatting to me as she used one hand to mix a large bowl full of the filling mixture, while the other kneaded the dough that would be used for the pastry cases. She was making a classic Kerala Jewish festival snack called pastels, made with shredded chicken pieces, fried with ginger, pepper, grated carrot, onions, cabbage and boiled eggs.

She rolled the dough out and then cut out round circles. In the centre of each circle she placed a spoonful of mixture and then sealed it in the shape of a semi-circle, creating a frilled border on one side. These would then be deep fried, a bit like *samosas*.

"This is for this evening. We'll take it to the synagogue tonight," she explained. "Tonight almost all of the Ernakulam Jews will be coming for prayers. The ones at Chennamangalam and Parul can't come because it's too far, but otherwise all the community will be there. You'll see." These two villages were also once Jewish strongholds, but now only a couple of families remained.

The Paradesi Synagogue was the only one that remained in proper service, with the other seven almost permanently out of use. So, on the days of major festivals, everyone would gather in Mattancherry for prayers, with some making a journey of almost two hours to get there. That morning the Ernakulam Jews had gone early to the Paradesi Synagogue for the first prayer service of the Shmini and Simchat Torah festival weekend, where they got to kiss the Torah. This evening, prior to sundown, they would honor the old tradition of lighting the candles on a metal tree to mark the festival of Shmini. This would be followed by prayers at seven thirty, after which the Jews could invite special guests to come inside the synagogue and view the special decorations. Prayers would continue on Saturday morning and evening and then again into Sunday. The new cycle for the Torah began the following week. It was one of the most demanding festivals of the year, but also one of the most happy of occasions.

"Every Jewish community celebrates Simhat Torah in its own way. In Bombay you'll see them celebrate it with great joy," said Ofra, nostalgic for her old city. "*There* you'll see the real happiness, the dancing and singing. Here you can't really see that. But tradition tells us to take the Torah and dance," she twirled in a circle, her flour-covered forearms lifted into the air in a moment of lightness as she demonstrated how one would embrace the holy book like a partner.

Ofra noted with amusement that not much dancing could be seen in Cochin these days as the Jews were mostly too elderly and weak to carry the heavy scrolls. In the old days, strapping men from the community would carry the heavy scrolls in their cases and literally cavort around the courtyard, leaping high and dancing as the other Jews followed behind singing and clapping. Grainy black and white photos from the heyday depict a riotous celebration of the holy book, with worshippers high on bottles of strong spirits known as "petrol" to give the occasion lift-off. Bottles of "petrol" were swigged early in the morning before going to synagogue and it was not unknown for some to secrete their own supply into the courtyard itself to fortify themselves during the drawn out prayers and proceedings. Tomorrow the Mattancherry Jews would dance with one symbolic Torah, but I imagined at their age it would be more of a stately waltz.

With the pastels prepared, she cleared the table and set it for lunch. Babu was back from the aquarium and beamed his welcome. His wife laid down an array of dishes as if by magic: chicken curry with the tiny sweet potatoes I had seen in the market, rice, a special dish of diced chicken pieces fried in a *masala* batter, salad and homemade pickle.

Babu explained each dish and pointed out the best bits to try. The two explained how when they first married, it had taken some time for Ofra to adjust to the change of pace from Bombay. It had been something of a gamble to leave behind everything for the village life of Kerala. At first she found it tough adjusting to the slower pace and the difference in food and climate. Bombay was a glamorous, cosmopolitan city set on a glittering emerald sea. Cochin was unhurried, provincial, a place where the idea of a night out was an evening of bridge with the elders. The tight-knit community, the suppurating humidity of these wet lowlands made for a claustrophobic life for a newlywed from Bombay. But they started a family and were happy. Babu was still amused whenever he recalled her shock at leaving her "big Bombay life". Why stay and not migrate to Israel, I asked.

"I did go to Israel, just to see," he replied. "I stayed there for a month or so to see if we could live there. If I liked it then I would take the family. But I decided we couldn't live there."

"Why?"

"I hated it. I found the Israelis arrogant. There's no love in their hearts for people like us. Here in India, the Malabari Jews are loved by all parts of the community. There I felt like the outsider. Maybe it's because of the way they live there—modern society, too fast, where there's no time for tradition, the synagogue, community. There it's work, spend, eat, sleep. *Bus.*

"They're closed in mind, closed in heart. Perhaps, because of the troubles they face. The political troubles, I mean. Enemies on each side. Living in siege. Always fearing the outsider, always fearing the dark face. I couldn't let my family live like this—fearing what might happen."

The sacrifice was too much. The Jews of Kerala had never known the persecution, the fear, the intolerance that other Diaspora communities faced through the ages. Instead, theirs had been a gilded existence. The

Ernakulam Jews in particular were closely integrated with the Hindus, Muslims and Christians. Babu was mindful of just how much they had to lose.

"Here in India, in Kerala, we're accepted and loved by all. We're safe. Why change this? When I got on the plane to leave Israel, even though this is my Holy Land, I was happy to be coming home. You know that smell when you step off the plane in India? That dirty diesel smell! You smell you're home. This smell," and tears welled in his eyes as he smiled, "I can't tell you how happy I was to breathe my country into my lungs. I'm Jewish. But I'm also Indian. What's Israel to me? It's a foreign country."

Then why did the Black Jews not share the same depth of despair as the White Jews, despite knowing that this was the end for them too in India?

"They're all old now, their youngsters are gone. Who's left to make them happy? All their lives, they wanted to be exclusive. Now they have their wish. They're excluded from everything."

The Malabari Jews, he said, had always been closer to the Indian mentality. "Throughout history we mixed with the other communities, we're part of them, they're part of us. We belong here still. There's life here still. Plus, we have young children with us. Only problem—who will they marry?"

"Will they go to Israel to find a husband, your girls?" His expression darkened again.

"The older daughter only has NASA Space Station on her mind. Not Cochin, the universe. The younger one is happy to stay here forever. What's for them in Israel? My sister was one of those who made the *aliyah*, the pilgrimage to Israel. She wanted a new life, a new beginning.

She went many years ago, married an Israeli and they had four children there."

"How does she like it?"

"My sister's now divorced. Her husband left them. This is their way there. This is *her* Israel," he said, the hard flat edge discernible in his voice again.

Suddenly, Babu began to weep uncontrollably, cupping his right hand over his eyes as teardrops rolled down his cheeks and into his food. Ofra tenderly placed her hand on his arm. I sensed Babu was crying for more than his sister's sadness. Eventually he smiled, as if embarrassed by such foolishness, wiped his eyes with the back of his hand and began to resume eating again, his right hand kneading the rice into a small tight ball and placing it into his mouth, continuing the meal in silence.

For Babu, Israel had not been the Promised Land. He had been one of many who went with expectations of finding a sense of belonging, of finally coming home after a history of rejection by fellow White Jews in India. But his *aliyah* had not provided any answers nor erased the yearning of those Black Jews who left to find acceptance. Instead he found an Israel torn asunder by religious insecurity, a land where peace was a stranger. For his sister and even for himself on that one brief visit, Israel did not turn out to be the fabled paradise that held them spellbound in childhood, but a hostile landscape of loneliness and rejection. India, for all its failings, remained home.

* * * *

CHAPTER FIVE

Land of Black Gold and White Pearls

"What strange tales would history unfold if the gift of speech was allowed to the stones and pebbles that lie embedded in the bosom of the river that flows by the once famous Cranganore?"

—K.P.P. MENON, *HISTORY OF KERALA*

From the inception of their community on the shores of Malabar two thousand or more years ago, the Cochini Jews never forgot they were the people of Israel and that this was only an interim homeland. Israel was invoked in prayer almost daily, toasted at festivals with the best whisky or *arrack*, toddy made with cashews.

The court of Solomon, the fall of the Second Temple and Jerusalem some thousand years later and the resulting forced migration was not merely the stuff of abstract antiquity but part of their very being. In view of this, it is clear that Babu's tears did not spring from sentimentality—he was a tough and pragmatic man after all—but originated in a profound sense of rejection, akin to a long-lost son finding no instinctive embrace from a father on his return.

Understanding that story is part of deciphering who they are. Elements of a lost Jerusalem were evoked in the ten windows of the synagogue which represented the commandments, the two pillars that flanked the Ark which were inspired by the destroyed Temple of Solomon, the hangings that adorned the synagogue walls which shared the sacred colors used in the ancient holy of holies. Each detail, down to the last carved flower, was a reminder of city where it began. The synagogue was a manifestation of faith to replace Israel until it was recovered. Therefore, there could be no greater agony than when the Black Jews were barred from worship in the Paradesi synagogue—it echoed the darkness and estrangement of the past.

* * * *

It was during the golden days of King Solomon's rule that the first contact was made between Israel and India. By the time Solomon took the throne in 970 BCE he had inherited from his father, David, a significant regional empire. Jerusalem was no longer a minor city-cum-state but the capital of this empire. To mark its ascendancy in status and power, Solomon embarked upon an ambitious building program that included a royal acropolis near Mount Zion, a palace and other grand architectural statements such as the House of the Forest of Lebanon. There was a treasury and the Judgment Hall, which housed Solomon's ivory throne as well as a separate palatial residence for his most politically important and illustrious wife, the daughter of the pharaoh.

But the most significant structure of all was the Temple to Yahweh, which came to be known as the Temple of Solomon. No physical trace of this first temple survived its destruction by the King of Babylon Nebuchadnezzar in 586 BCE, but it lives on almost three millennia after it was first constructed through biblical accounts that lavish the reader with every minute detail of its structure. It remains ever present in the spiritual landscape of the Jewish people, symbolizing an era in their history when God dwelled among them in the house that Solomon built.

The Temple of Solomon contained the Ark of the Covenant, a chest which held the tablets of Law handed down to Moses. Mounted upon the Ark were two golden cherubim whose wings fanned outwards to form a throne for Yahweh. This throne symbolized the presence of the divine among his people, an indication that Yahweh himself sat in the midst of his worshippers. Responsibility for carrying the Ark had always been in the hands of the tribe of Levi, a caste of priests of whom Moses' brother, Aaron, was chief. Its stewardship was of the highest importance and its care entrusted to a select few. The Ark was believed to be possessed of a terrible sacred power that would protect the Jewish people against their enemies, helping to smite them in battle.

The Ark was the only symbol of a divine presence in the Temple that contained no effigies in accordance with God's instruction to Moses during his revelation in the burning bush, where he declared he must not be defined by any human form. While it remained in the Temple it was seen by the Jewish people as a spiritual epicenter that directly connected mortal life to heaven, to God himself.

Apart from this distinctive feature of the Ark, the Temple conformed to typical imperial architecture of the region. In the courtyard in front of the Temple stood an altar of sacrifice as well as a huge bronze basin representing Yam, the primal sea. This alluded to the forces of darkness or chaos, a reminder of how the Jewish people had escaped slavery in Egypt.

The main temple entrance was flanked by the pillars and its walls, both inside and out, were etched with angels and cherubs, almonds and flowers and swaying palm trees. A central staircase led up to the main *Ulam* or vestibule, which in turn led through to the *Hekhal* or cult hall at the eastern end of the building. Another flight of stairs separated this chamber from the *Devir* or Holy of Holies, which contained the Ark itself, screened from view by a curtain of blue, crimson and purple. These same colors are seen to this day in the Paradesi Synagogue's central chamber.

One cannot over-emphasize the significance of the Temple of Solomon to the faithful, then as well as now. Coming to the Temple, abode of Yahweh himself, was entering the sanctuary of one's faith. Solomon was also seen as a special king in the hearts of the Jewish people, for God had granted *him* the honor of building a Temple in his name. The king of the Jews was a ruler anointed by God: his palace resided next to the house of God, his seat of power was beside Yahweh's own throne on the Ark. In Karen Armstrong's *A History of Jerusalem* she describes the duty of the leader of the Jewish people to impart justice: "If this justice prevailed there would be peace, harmony and fertility in the kingdom," she said. "Yahweh would provide them with the security which was so earnestly and continually sought for in the ancient world . . . But there was no security and no *shalom* if there was no justice in Zion."

Shalom meant more than just peace, it signified a spiritual wholeness and harmony with the world. Maybe this Jewish understanding of linking justice to *shalom* lay at the root of the sense of retribution that the latter day Jews of Cochin felt had befallen their own kingdom in India. During the course of the history of the Jews of Kerala, justice had not always prevailed.

While Solomon was revered for his wisdom and for giving the Jewish people the first temple, in the end justice and *shalom* evaded his kingdom as it came under mounting strain because of the heavy financial cost of his building program, which proved a drain on national resources and required large-scale conscripted labor. As Solomon built his glittering new Jerusalem, the demand for luxuries with which to furnish it became ever greater. It opened up an era of seafaring voyages from Israel to India. Biblical accounts indicate trade fleets first making contact with India's coastal region during this time as Solomon's men sought out exotic treasures to bring back to his kingdom.

In *The Last Jews of Cochin: Jewish Identity in Hindu India*, Nathan Katz and Ellen Goldberg noted that the Hebrew Bible contained a number of words which were very similar to Sanskrit and Tamil, suggesting there were indeed established links between Solomon's kingdom and India. They added that the First Book of Kings indicated the opulence of the court of King Solomon was partly attributable to this trade, bringing imported luxuries such as ivory, apes and peacocks.

Other historians also flagged up these Biblical clues. In *The Jews of Kerala*, P.M. Jussay said that while there were no reliable records on when Jews first arrived in Kerala, it is believed that the earliest Jews were sailors from King Solomon's ships, which according to the Bible brought "once every three years, silver, elephant's tooth, peacocks and apes."

The Bible's word for peacock is "tukiyum" and for apes it is "kapim". The Tamil words for peacock and ape are "tokai" and "kapi", respectively, says Jussay. The ancient Roman chronicles of Pliny the Elder and The Periplus of the Erythraean Sea also provide evidence of maritime trade between the Red Sea coast and Muziris, another name for Cranganore.

So began the first contact between the two countries, as trading partners. The region of southern India, where Tamil was spoken, was on the map of Solomon's kingdom, according to these sources. The verbal history of the Jews of Cochin said some of these first merchant traders and their slaves may have settled on the coastline of Kerala.

The first Jews to land on this coast were probably part of that trading community. As such, historians believe the Jews who arrived on trading ships were unlikely to have traveled with their families. Local rulers would have provided these foreign customers with lodging and the Jews would have become involved with local women, since they were far from home. The resulting children would form the beginnings of the Jewish community in Kerala.

A further trickle of settlers came to India several centuries after Solomon's rule, at the time of the destruction of the first temple in 586 BCE by the Babylonian ruler Nebuchadnezzar. In a merciless assault, Jerusalem was sacked and the Temple of Solomon was gutted of its precious furnishings and burned to the ground. The contents of the temple were taken to Babylon, but the fate of the Ark was not recorded. It simply vanished from history. The inauspicious disappearance of the seat of Yahweh was interpreted as a sign that God had deserted the Jewish people. The Jewish people were exiles, with many having to protect their faith in the land of their new master, Babylon. Others reportedly fled to further flung lands, including India.

The loss of the temple was a devastating blow. The earthly seat of God had been razed, their holy kingdom transformed into wasteland and their people scattered. There was no longer a physical manifestation of the spiritual epicenter of their faith. The link between heaven and earth had been severed.

But the hope of returning and rebuilding their Jerusalem was not extinguished. Instead, in their period of banishment, these first exiles sought to preserve the purity of their faith: keeping the Sabbath, circumcising their male children and so on. They remained distinct from non-Jews. These were the outwards signs of the Jews being a holy people. By refusing to relinquish their faith and maintaining their separateness, the hope of return to Israel was kept alive and eventually realized by some. Indeed, the same mentality was adopted by the Cochin Jews during their time in India.

By 520 BCE the foundations of the Second Temple in Jerusalem had been laid and on the Jewish feast of Sukkoth a special dedication ceremony was held by the priests. This new manifestation lacked the magnificence of the Temple of Solomon and it no longer housed the sacred Ark, but it did resurrect hope. It would be some 500 years later in 19 BCE that Herod decided to fully restore the Second Temple, returning it to something approaching the resplendence of the first. To ensure the holy site was not polluted by ordinary men, he had a thousand priests trained as masons and carpenters so that they could take responsibility for the Hekhal and Devir. In such a way the new temple was completed. It was a glorious return.

The Second Temple drew huge numbers of pilgrims during the time of Herod's rule, with as many as half a million coming to the major feast days such as Passover and Sukkoth. The atmosphere at these times was one of enormous jubilation. On the special festival of Sukkoth or Tabernacles, marking the Israelites' period in the desert after their Exodus from Egypt, each Jewish family would prepare a sacrificial lamb at the Temple. The ecstasy of return after exile, of seeing their temple resurrected to its former glory, was a remarkable reversal of fortune for the Jewish people.

But it would not last. By 70 CE the Jews were crushed into submission once again. In that year the Romans laid siege to Jerusalem and broke into the Temple's inner courts. Six thousand Jewish zealots lay in wait, willing to lay down their lives to defend their beloved Temple. Even in the face of death, they were careful to safeguard the purity laws associated with the Temple chambers.

In his writings, the second-century Greek historian Dio Cassius described the incredible fortitude of the Jewish faithful: "The ordinary people fought in the forecourt and the nobility in the inner courts while the priests defended the Temple building itself." It was to no avail, and when the Jews saw the Second Temple ablaze they uttered agonizing cries of despair, with some of those present throwing themselves upon the sword of the enemy or plunging into the flames rather than live to see their Temple destroyed.

The Temple was smashed to pieces by Roman troops and only the Western Wall of the Devir remained standing. The wall is all that survives to this day and it is the most sacred place for Jews around the world. Even now, the memory of the Temple's destruction has the power to move its people to tears and plunge them into grief anew. When I visited the Western Wall, or Wailing Wall as it is also known, the sheer force of reawakened sorrow and despair were palpable: people would come to the wall to pray and then without warning their bodies would crumple before its towering presence, fingertips clinging onto the pale yellow brickwork as they wept into the stones.

The Jewish people were left in no doubt about their position after the fall of Jerusalem and the Temple. After 70 CE there was a Roman coin in circulation that depicted a Jewess with hands bound tight as she sat under a palm tree. An order was issued to the Romans to hunt down and execute any Jew who claimed to descend from King David. Jewish property was confiscated and many were driven out. Their people faced humiliation and a kind of religious emasculation in their own city. The temple taxes extracted from male Jews by the Romans were donated to the Temple of Jupiter in Rome. Roman soldiers would make sacrifices to their gods in Jerusalem's streets. The Jewish holy city was defiled and the debris of the Temple was polluted by the blood of its own people.

Even decades after the destruction, the Jewish people remained in a state of shock and spiritual paralysis, with the Book of Baruch saying that nature itself should succumb to a period of mourning:

> *"For why should light rise again*
> *Where the light of Zion is darkened?"*

In the period after the fall of Jerusalem, Jews were again expelled from their holy city and their fortunes scattered to foreign winds. Again, they were exiles.

It was to this juncture in history that the Cochini Jews attributed the arrival of the first large-scale community of Jewish migrants from Israeli to Indian soil. The Kerala coastline was already on the map of the Jewish people due to trading links that went back almost a millennium. Now in their moment of desperation, the Jews of Israel came not as merchant traders, but as refugees. How could they know it would be millennia before they returned?

This is seen as the pivotal moment in Cochini Jewish history, providing the crucial link between the sacred city of Jerusalem and what would become a substitute Jerusalem in India, the port city of

Cranganore. Out of the fire and devastation of Jerusalem, this community of Jews was delivered on the west coast of Kerala.

* * * *

It is remarkable that India should have been a natural choice of refuge
for the Jews during this tumultuous period. Various factors point to why
this is so. Trade was well established between Israel and India from the
time of Solomon, according to old Hebrew and Biblical accounts, as described above, but this was given fresh impetus by 45 CE with the dis-
covery of the monsoon winds by Hippalus, which cut the sea journey to
India dramatically.

The Indian community was well looked upon in Jewish society, it
would appear. Josephus describes in his chronicles that in Israel during the
time of the destruction of the Second Temple, there was some knowledge
of Hindu philosophy. He made the astonishing revelation that the Hindu
attitude towards life and death was discussed by a group of Jewish zealots
just before the mass martyrdom of Masada in 73 CE, according to Katz
and Goldberg. In Josephus' account of the speech of the leader of the rebels,
Eleazar, he used Hindu philosophy towards death. In Hinduism, death is
seen as merely part of the ongoing cycle of destruction and rebirth. He
drew upon this to persuade his soldiers to embrace martyrdom:

"We . . . ought to become an example to others of our readiness
to die. Yet if we do stand in need of foreigners to support us in
this matter, let us regard those Indians . . . These have such a
desire of a life of immortality that they tell other men before-

hand that they are about to depart and nobody hinders them but every one thinks them happy men . . ."

Josephus said the Masada Jews were swayed by his argument and martyrdom proceeded. The writer William Whitson concurs with the theory that Hindu beliefs had permeated early Jewish culture: "How was there knowledge of Indian beliefs and practices? Josephus is described by some scholars as a Hellenized Jew with knowledge of Greek historians who held Indian philosophy in high regard."

So Hindu culture was already part of Jewish consciousness and, in turn, the Keralites welcomed foreigners to their shores, seeing them as a source of revenue and skills which enhanced the regional economy.

Around this time, the Romans already had connections on the Malabar coast and had established a colony at Muziris. In 60 CE, The Periplus of the Erythraean Sea, a mariners' guide to the Red Sea and Indian Ocean, described the scene: "Muziris . . . abounds in ships sent there with cargoes from Arabia and by the Greeks . . . Kings send large ships to those market towns on account of the great quantity and bulk of pepper."

Ships came loaded with gold in their cargos and returned with holds bursting with black pepper. Such exchanges ensured that it swiftly entrenched its position as a wealthy port city and cosmopolitan hub with a rather raffish air. The great classical second-century Tamil poem the *Shilappadikaram*, or Lay of the Ankle Bracelet, portrays a city glinting with foreign gold, where "lusty sailors sang" and "all night, lamps were burning, the lamps of foreigners who talk strange tongues, who watch over precious cargoes near the docks."

Against this energizing backdrop of fast-expanding trade and migration from Israel, Greece, Syria and Rome, Jews arrived over the centuries that followed the fall of Jerusalem to establish their first large-scale settlement in Kerala. The earliest Jewish settlements were in Calicut and Quilon. But Cranganore remains the most important of all. The settlement of Jews on the northern side of Cranganore was at Pullot, where there was a temple ferry. The word "ferry" in Malayalam is "kadavu" and so the Jewish settlement came to be known as Kadavumbagam or "the ferry side". The Jewish settlement on the southern bank of the River Periyar was known as Tekkumbagam—these communities were made up of poorer Jews who were involved in the docks or as commercial agents.

There was also a settlement at Cherigandaram, made up of Jewish merchants. It was in this area that Joseph Rabban settled after being conferred with princely privileges by the local raja. These rights, sometimes described as the Cochini Jews' Magna Carta, were set out on the engraved copper plates that now lie with the Paradesi Jews in their synagogue. The plates have been dated as late as 1000 BC by historians.

This was a time of the Chera-Chola conflict in the south and during a crisis point in the war the Chera King, Bhaskara Ravi Varma, convened a war council of the governors of the provinces, his commander-in-chief and regional leaders. It is believed that Rabban agreed to help, placing assets and men at his disposal and so the king raised the status of the Jewish settlement to an autonomous entity and made Rabban the head, granting the seventy-two privileges. Rabban's reward for such fealty was a kingdom of his own, in perpetuity.

Cochin's line of Hindu kings would honor the deal struck with Rabban and the Jews were held in extremely high regard, even centuries on.

This close relationship between the Jews and the raja of the princely state is seen to be unique within India, according to numerous historical accounts. The other Jewish communities in the Indian cities of Bombay and Calcutta were successful businessmen but did not have the same political privileges bestowed by the local ruling power.

Until Independence in 1947 the Jews benefited from a number of privileges in Cochin, which remained a Hindu princely state until the British left India. For example, Jewish holidays were observed and the banks were closed on Rosh Hashanah and Yom Kippur. Exams were never held for Jewish students on Shabbat and they were given a seat on the legislative council of the state of Cochin, even though they did not have a big enough population to justify this. Jews were also allocated a certain number of places at medical and law school.

Today, where Cranganore once stood there is little trace of its momentous history. Most of the ancient city was destroyed in periodic attacks by Arab and Portuguese soldiers. But something of the magic of those early years is conveyed in Tamil poetry from the second century that described a city "surrounded by a moat."

"On the surface of the water floated large lotus flowers, red and white water lilies and the blue iris," it said. The residential quarters were graced with "wide avenues" where guards watched over "rich dwellings". There were parks with trees and flowers and "pools with such limpid water that the inhabitants of heaven left their paradise to visit these banks."

In his *History of Kerala*, K.P.P. Menon marvels at the heritage of Cranganore in not just Jewish, but world history. It was here that Solomon's ships alighted; here that St. Thomas first arrived in India in 52 AD, planted a cross and preached Christianity, according to Kerala tradition. Here that numerous trading powers, from the Chinese and Arabs to the Portuguese and Dutch arrived with lofty ambitions of conquest and commerce. Yet, today, its crumbling relics are the abode of howling jackals, Menon lamented. "The old moat is the haunt of crocodiles and paddy birds."

Some clues of the past remain. One of the earliest Jewish accounts of Malabar was written by the merchant Benjamin of Tudela, who chronicled life of Jewish communities across the world. Writing about the Malabar coastal region, he described the stupefying heat of an Indian summer:

> "From Passover to New Year . . . no man can go out of his house because of the sun, for the heat in that country is intense. Everybody remains in his house until the evening. They go forth and kindle lights in all the market places and all the street and do their work and business at nighttime. For they have to turn night into day in consequence of the great heat of the sun."

Turning to the Jewish community of Malabar in particular, he describes "only about one hundred Jews who were of Black color as well as the other inhabitants. The Jews are good men, observers of the law and possess the Pentateuch; the people have some little knowledge of the Talmud."

Further flashes of life are provided by the "Cairo Genizah documents", a collection of 250,000 documents stored in the anteroom of a synagogue in Old Cairo. Genizah means "hiding place" in Hebrew, and when the archive was discovered in 1896 there were documents spanning several hundred years, giving an insight into Jewish life in the Middle Ages, including missives written by Jewish merchants who started to

travel between the Mediterranean and China in the ninth century, stopping along Malabar's coast.

Translated by Shlomo D. Goitein, the letters regarding India painted
a vivid picture: of the homesickness of the traders who missed family life,
how they savored the kosher cheeses sent as a gift from their partners in
Alexandria and Aden; how the men lapsed into using concubines during
their long leaves of absence. The archive is a window into past lives. For
example, some seventy fragments portray the life of a Tunisian-born Jew
called Abraham Ben Yiju. He set off to make his fortune in Indian trade
in the 1120s. The documents depict the small triumphs and tragedies
that make up a lifetime. His correspondence tells of a difficult journey, his
business dealings and marriage to an Indian slave girl called Ashu; his
acumen in the import-export business—he exported iron and spices to
his Jewish partners in Aden while importing arsenic, paper and other
commodities to India; the birth of his three children and then the premature death of his young son in India.

The documents relating to Ben Yiju tell one of the most important
histories of the Jews who migrated and worked in India. He was a highly
educated merchant, noted for his scholarship and calligraphy. His correspondence to Aden illustrated the type of trade that existed with India
at the time. There was some suggestion that he also traded slaves. He
opened a brass factory on the Malabar coast at one point, which employed local Jews as well as others.

Clearly, he was well regarded by his business partners. One letter
from a trading associate in Aden acknowledging the receipt of a shipment
of black pepper concludes with the following gushing sentiments: "The
letter of my lord, the most illustrious elder has arrived; may God make

permanent your well being, may he guard your life and humble those who envy you."

After spending some eighteen years in India, he left in 1149 to return to Aden only to find many of his family had left the country. He received a frosty reception from the Jewish community who questioned the validity of his marriage. His homecoming was a less than happy one.

Marco Polo also traveled to the region during the late thirteenth century and mentioned the kingdom of what is now Quilon on Malabar's coast: "It is the residence of many Christians and Jews, who retain their proper language," he said in his travelogue. "The king is not a tributary to any other."

"The heat during some months is so violent as to be scarcely supportable; yet the merchants resort thither from various parts of the world . . . attracted by great profits."

Cranganore was famous not just for commodities but for precious stones such as diamonds, rubies and pearls that were in much demand by rich Roman ladies. In his chronicles *Naturalis Historia*, the Roman military commander, philosopher and writer, Pliny the Elder, made clear his disapproval of the appetite for such fripperies from what he called "India's first emporium": "Our ladies glory in having pearls suspended from their fingers, one, two or three of them dangling from their ears, delighted even with the rattling of pearls as they knock against each other; and now, the poorer classes are even affecting them as people are in the habit of saying 'a pearl worn by a woman in public is as good as a lector walking before her'", said the Roman military chief.

Pliny was equally disapproving of the insatiable appetite for black pepper among his countrymen, clearly fearing it would drain Rome's coffers dry: "Both pepper and ginger grow wild . . . and yet we buy them by weight like silver and gold," he sniffed.

Nose-tickling bounties of pepper known as "black gold"; exquisite shawls and turbans embellished with silver thread; luminescent pearls and corals harvested from the sea bed, perfumed camphor wood and oils destined to grace the boudoir of some fragrant foreign matron. These were the treasures that drove men from the sanctuary of family life to perilous sea voyages, ushering them to the heat-induced madness of Malabar summers and into the arms of their velvet-eyed lovers.

Such was the scene at a time when Cranganore was the most important of cities in the region. As already established, the city was not just a trading center but a place imbued with religious significance. What would drive them from such a place?

The old Shingly songs, the musical history of the people, hinted at quarrels over funds for the synagogue that led to a rupture in the Jewish leadership. But in 1341, it was nature, not man, that decided the fate of the Cranganore Jews and changed the course of the community. As a result of a torrential downpour of rain, the River Periyar flooded, silting up the harbor mouth. Because of this biblical-style flood Cranganore lost its strategic maritime position. A new harbor formed at Cochin that was smaller than the last but would replace Cranganore as the regional port. It was called Kochazhi or "small estuary" which eventually became known as Kochi or Cochin.

Faced with this natural disaster, the first party of Jews left for Cochin. The Jews settled in swiftly. Indeed, by 1345 a synagogue was built there. It was known as the Kochangadi synagogue and the first outside of Cranganore.

These people marked the first wave of migration from the old settlement. As Cochin's importance rose in the region, so Cranganore's declined. The Jews who remained in the old city over the next two centuries found their power and influence diminish as trade switched to Cochin. The kingdom of Cochin, under the raja, found itself at loggerheads with the local dominant power at Calicut in the north, whose rulers were known as the Zamorins.

It was the Zamorins who first had contact with the Portuguese with the arrival of Vasco da Gama in the fifteenth century. At the time the Arabs dominated this lucrative trade route and the Portuguese were keen to take over. In Correa's *Three Voyages*, which describes the Portuguese assault on the Malabar Coast, there is a fascinating description of da Gama's first encounter with the ruler of Zamorin at Calicut. He looked every inch the European dandy when he was received at the royal court.

"[He was dressed] in a long cloak, coming down to his feet, of tawny colored satin, lined with smooth brocade and underneath a short tunic of blue satin and white buskins and on his head a cap of blue velvet with a white feather fastened with a splendid medal; and a valuable enamel collar on his shoulders and a rich sash with a handsome dagger." The king received him "seated on a rich bed set out with silk and gold", wearing bracelets studied with jewels, including a diamond as thick as his thumb. Around his neck were pearls "the size of hazelnuts" and a necklace of rubies and emeralds.

Da Gama wanted to secure a trade agreement, but the king was noncommittal. Relations deteriorated when the Portuguese were requested to pay customs to the port where their ships were docked, before departing. Da Gama refused and simply left. He returned to Portugal to report his findings and was hailed as a hero for discovering the sea route. He had come bearing goods worth sixty times the cost of the voyage, so plans were made for an armada of thirty-three ships to return. This time the person in charge was Pedro Alvarez Cabral, a man of "overweening pride" who perceived insults in every innocent gesture, according to *Malabar and the Portuguese* by K.M. Panikkar, published in 1929. He had "neither tact nor foresight," said Panikkar. On arrival, he made the fundamental error of sending a low born fisherman to give a message to the sovereign, which was interpreted as a great insult in caste-based India. After a rocky start, the Portuguese finally got permission to build a factory in Calicut. But the initial ill omens were realized.

The Portuguese believed they now had the right to the trade route and saw themselves as the new heirs to the seas of the region, with the right to confiscate goods of those who sailed there without their permission. This belief led to Cabral seizing an Arab ship in harbor because they were loading pepper he wanted for himself. He did not believe natives had the right to sell to whoever paid the best price. The news angered the locals, unused to such aggressive tactics. A riot ensued and the factory was destroyed and many Portuguese were wounded.

Da Gama responded by massacring the crew of all other boats and burning their ships. The rulers decided the Portuguese were "uncivilized barbarians, treacherous, untrustworthy". The Zamorin and Portuguese were now enemies. Sensing danger, Cabral was advised by a Jew turned Christian in his crew, Gaspar da India, that he should sail to Cochin. He reached there on Christmas Eve in 1500. There he sought an audience with the local raja and he was granted permission to buy all he wished. A treaty was drawn up and permission granted to build another factory.

At that time the raja of Cochin was fearful of the powerful Zamorin and saw the Portuguese as potential allies in his bid for freedom. In the end, the raja simply exchanged one bondage for another as the Portuguese governor assumed the position of colonial overlord. The Portuguese would build garrisons in their new base, as well as more factories. But their old enemy plagued their ambitions for expansion.

The Calicut rulers wanted vengeance on the foreign invader and in the years that followed a war raged with the Portuguese and their new ally, the raja of Cochin. Once the Jews moved from Cranganore to Cochin, they too would be embroiled in this bloody intrigue.

The Zamorins together with their allies the Arabs also wanted to expand their territory beyond Calicut, leading to clashes with the Jews of Cranganore as well as the Portuguese.

In 1524 the feuding between the Jews and Arabs of Cranganore reached a flashpoint when a row broke over the adulteration of the supply of pepper which led to the death of a Muslim. Angry and looking for a fight, the Muslims gathered and attacked the Jews, killing some of their number, burning their houses and synagogues. The Calicut rulers gave their blessing to the attack.

It was too much for the remaining Jews of Cranganore to bear and another wave migrated to Cochin. So the Jewish people were now scattered across numerous communities in Cochin. Having lost the old settlement given to them centuries earlier, they were given sanctuary by his descendant, the Hindu raja of Cochin, who allotted them parcels of land that would become known as the Jew Towns of Mattencherry and Ernakulam.

By the seventeenth century there were synagogues across Ernakulam and Cochin. In the case of the Malabari Jews, the new synagogues took on the names of the old Cranganore predecessors in order to keep tradition alive. While Cochin was to become forever associated with the Jewry of the region, Cranganore remained their spiritual homeland in India. The very last of the Jews had left Cranganore around 1566. By this time the Portuguese were well established on the western coastline and in Cochin, with ambitions to turn it into the most important trading port of the region. From 1503 to 1663 the Portuguese were the dominant foreign power in Cochin, where the raja remained a titular head. The Portuguese turned out to be cruel overlords, persecuting the Jewish people until the Dutch displaced them.

It was in the sixteenth century that the final major wave of Jewish immigrants came from overseas to join the older communities that hailed from Cranganore. The newcomers were escaping the horrors of the Inquisition in Europe. In an essay, "The Cochin Jews of Kerala," the historian Barbara Johnson says that some were Sephardic Jews, direct as well as indirect refugees from the Spanish and Portuguese expulsions. Others came via Constantinople, Aleppo and other Middle Eastern territories.

Reports indicated that some of this wave of refugees came as families, but the single men among them married some of the Jewish women from the so-called "first families" of Cranganore. In 1568, the newcomers known as the Paradesis or "foreigners" in Malayalam built a synagogue on the plot of land next to the raja's palace in Cochin. Johnson said in her essay: "They adopted the Malayalam language and identified enthusiastically with Kerala customs and traditions, but at some point they stopped marrying the Jews who had been there many centuries before them. In written accounts, the Paradesis were referred to as 'white Jews' and the more ancient Malabari communities as 'black Jews', though there is not always a clear distinction between them in terms of skin color."

In the early years of Cochini life, the two communities came together and in some cases intermarried. Fleeing the brutality and persecution of the inquisitors of Europe, the Paradesi Jews quickly assimilated into life in India. Unlike Jews elsewhere in the world, they found acceptance among the natives and the existing Jewish community. It started with promise, so what changed to create a fissure that would take centuries to repair?

* * * *

As a community, the Jews had to delicately tiptoe through the minefield of colonial politics for ascendancy in the region. In 1662, the Jews united with the Dutch against the hated Portuguese who had targeted them mercilessly. During their time on India's west coast, the Portuguese would use force to convert locals to Christianity and even introduced the Inquisition in neighboring Goa in the early sixteenth century. Goa would eventually become the Portuguese epicenter for trade.

Until then, the Jews of Cochin found themselves in the firing line for their faith and allegiance to the Dutch in 1662. The Portuguese exacted their revenge by burning the synagogue, Torah scrolls and records and then sacked Jew Town. But by 1663 the Dutch had defeated the Portuguese, opening up a period of benign colonial relations for the Jews, who enjoyed a renaissance of culture and trade. Cochin grew more prosperous and the Jews reaped the benefits of links with the rest of the Dutch empire through shipments of books and contacts with Jewish communities in Europe. The first British troops came to Malabar in 1615 but did not replace the Dutch as the dominant colonial power in Cochin until 1797. The British presence was confined to Fort Cochin and Willingdon Island.

In the centuries that followed the Jews' move to Cochin, they had to play a canny game, not just to survive as a minority community but also to exploit Cochin's significance on the world trading map.

The key advantage the Jews had was strong historic links to the royal family. Back to the days of Joseph Rabban, Jews had established close ties with the raja and joined his men in battle. The Cochini royal family never forgot the favor. The Jews lived on plots of land provided by the royal family and, in the case of the Paradesi Jews, were neighbors to the maharajah's palace. Therefore, who better to act as mediator between the ambitious trading powers and the royal family of Cochin?

The significance of Joseph Rabban in the history of Jewish-Indo relations meant that both sides—the older Malabari Jews and the Paradesis needed to claim him as their own. While the Whites and Blacks had initially integrated on some level, this was to change.

In their studies, Katz and Goldberg noted that the community split along color lines, reflecting the indigenous caste system of the Kerala Hindus. Although such caste divisions were a breach of Jewish law or *Halakha*, the practice became entrenched.

Anthropologist David Mandelbaum believed the distinction was introduced by the Jews from Europe and the Middle East, including those who fled religious persecution in Spain and Portugal in the sixteenth century. The new arrivals boasted of their Jewish lineage and greater Jewish knowledge compared to the Malabar Jews, who had been isolated from the rest of the world and therefore lacked the others' European sophistry.

There were two main sub-castes in the Cochini Jewry, based on whether one was considered to be descended from ancient Israel or not. Those who claimed to hail from Israel were deemed to be superior. The other key sign of superiority was a lineage going back to Cranganore—those Jews who traced back to Rabban were seen to have a distinguished ancestry that went back to a line of kings. Therefore, they had a higher status in Indian society.

Cochini Jewish scholars note that the Paradesi Jews introduced a racial element, whereby skin color was also seen to be a sign of religious purity. The Paradesis claimed they were the only pure Jews of Kerala, pointing to their pale skin as evidence, and also laid claim to links with Cranganore. The Malabari Jews, far from being the inheritors of the King of Shingly, were the offspring of slave converts according to the Paradesis' version of history.

Mandelbaum, one of the most respected authorities on the subject, said it was impossible to uphold the claim that the Cranganore Jews had no mixed blood. Those Jewish merchants and crew who came to Malabar from the time of Solomon were unlikely to have made the dangerous journey with wives and children in tow, he said. So it is likely that they married and lived with local women. These local women gave birth to their children, who became Jews. If this was so, then where did that leave the Paradesis' claim of Jewish purity as well as Cranganore ancestry?

The truth lay in events that happened centuries ago, if not millennia. Much of the history was based on narrative and there was no documentation to prove that the White Jewish community had never intermarried with the locals when they first arrived. Yet, this claim of purity of ancestry, purity of Jewishness, was something which led the Paradesis to claim a natural ascendancy.

In caste-based India, where the concept of religious purity is paramount, the taint of slavery eventually undermined the Malabaris' standing in the royal court of Cochin. Loss of status and economic influence was only part of the cost they had to bear. Dubbed the sons of slaves, the Black Jews would be barred from marrying the White Jews, barred from the Paradesi synagogue, barred from forming their own place of worship in their homes.

It is true that such color-based divisions existed even among other Jewish communities in India, such as the Bene Israel community in Bombay. But in Cochin it was highly institutionalized. Indeed, the issue was on the radar of rabbis of the fifteenth and sixteenth century, who ruled it was wrong to discriminate against the Black Jews. In 1520, Rabbi David ben Solomon ibn Zimra wrote a letter in Hebrew from Cairo. In it, he noted there was a smaller group known as the "meyuchasim" or Jews "with a pedigree" who refused to mix with the other Jewish community whom they referred to as "slaves."

When asked for rabbinical advice on intermarriage, the Cochini Jews were told that intermarriage between the two communities was allowed after a prayer ritual of conversion was performed—that would eliminate any doubts the white Jews had about the purity of the black community. Such a ritual would mean it was wrong to refer to the Black Jews as slaves. But the Rabbi's advice was ignored by the Paradesis.

The question in all this is: why create a divide among themselves when they had come to India to escape persecution in Europe? The answer was money and power. The Black Jews had it. The White Jews wanted it. Forty years after the petition to Rabbi ibn Zimra, the Paradesis' economic and social status rose as the other group's declined. The Paradesis had secured land from the king next to his palace to build a synagogue. They were in close proximity and in an ideal position to press their case. In the end, the Brahmin maharajah favored the fair skinned and "pure" minority.

In Solomon's time, the link between justice and *shalom* was seen to be inviolable. Without justice there could be no harmony, no fertility, no *shalom*. Cochin's division was to become known as the "Jewish apartheid", going against this very tenet of faith. Kerala's Jewry turned on one another. And it would take centuries of campaigning by the Black Jews and eventually a black civil rights leader known as the "Jewish Gandhi" to deliver justice in Cochin.

* * * *

CHAPTER SIX

Opium Traders and Oil Pressers: The Lost Tribes

"And it shall come to pass in that day
That the Lord will set his hand again the second time
To recover the remnant of His people . . ."

—ISAIAH 11:11

The Jews of Kerala are acknowledged as the oldest in India, yet there are others with an equally rich heritage. The first is the Bene Israel community, or "Sons of Israel", who are based in Bombay. The second is the Baghdadi Jews who have now all but disappeared. All three communities have been the subject of much speculation on whether they originated from Israel's Ten Lost Tribes who vanished into the ether of history almost three millennia ago. What happened to these tribes remains one of the mysteries of Judaism and the subject of eternal speculation.

Before his death, Moses bequeathed command of the twelve tribes of his people to Joshua who went on to conquer the land of Canaan around 1200 BCE, according to the Bible. The land was eventually divided between these tribes. Judah and Benjamin took the southern territories, which would become the Kingdom of Judah, while the remaining ten tribes took the land that would become the Kingdom of Israel. In 722 BCE, Israel fell to the Assyrians and its people were dispersed. What became of these lost tribes is unknown, yet the Biblical prophecies maintain the Jews safeguarded their religious identity in foreign lands and that one day they would be reunited in the Holy Land. The story of the Lost Tribes remains an inviolable belief for many Jews and continues to fascinate.

The mystery ensnared the imagination of chroniclers, with accounts of communities which survived despite their displacement in alien lands. In the arena of sacred mythology it is difficult to prove who is linked to the Lost Tribes, yet it has been suggested that the Jews of India are among them, alongside the Falashas of Ethiopia and Pathans of Afghanistan.

* * * *

Today the Bene Israel Jews are the largest community in India, with a fairly stable population of around 5,000 people. Tradition says they arrived in India sometime between the eighth and sixth century BCE. They were traveling along the western Konkan coast when their boat was shipwrecked during a storm near Navagaon, which lies some forty-eight kilometers south of modern-day Mumbai. The community claims only seven women and seven men survived the tragedy, with the rest perishing in the treacherous Arabian Sea. The few bodies that were recovered were buried in a cemetery at Navagaon. These seven original couples grew into a community of thousands and lived in rural Maharashtra.

There were differing theories on their origins. One was that they hailed from the Holy Land in the time of Elijah, which explained why that same prophet had a central place in their traditions. Another theory was they were Persian or Yemeni. Either way, the community found themselves in an alien landscape, hemmed in by streams and mountains. They faced the apocalyptic sight of their first Indian monsoon, when the sky turned black, coastal winds bent the palm trees into submission and an insufferable humidity descended, accompanied by ceaseless rains which engulfed everything, turning soil into slurry and causing roiling rivers to overwhelm their banks.

Yet they acclimatized and settled. They eventually took up oil pressing, adapting their traditional skill of using olives. They established farming practices as well as the cultivation of coconut groves and sold produce on. Others took up skilled work such as carpentry. The community would work for six days and on the Sabbath they rested. One account from 1917, *A Short Account of the Calcutta Jews, with a Sketch of the Bene Israels, the Cochin Jews, the Chinese Jews and the Black Jews of Abyssinia* by I.A. Isaac, described their plight thus:

> "Homeless, penniless, ignorant of the language of the country and unaccustomed to the scorching Indian sun, they took to agriculture and oil pressing. Their abstinence from work on Saturdays earned them the sobriquet of 'Sabbath oil pressers'".

In *The Jews of India*, published by the Israel Museum in Jerusalem, their religious rituals are described as being "based on biblical Judaism: they celebrated Jewish holidays related to the Bible; the Sabbath was strictly observed; all male children were circumcised eight days after birth."

Their guidance was provided by religious leaders called *kazis*, who officiated on Jewish matters and were often seen by local authorities as leaders who could deal with disputes. Initially, the community had no synagogue or Torah scrolls, replying purely upon their spiritual leaders.

By the seventeenth century, the British East India Company had established itself in Bombay, now called Mumbai. This acted as a catalyst for change as Bombay grew into the most important trading port in India and employment boomed, attracting thousands of people from across the subcontinent. One imagines the mood of expansion and boundless opportunity may be similar to the economic renaissance that India is witnessing right now, as millions migrate from the villages to the cities looking for a stake in the capitalist revolution.

In this same way, the Bene Israel people also migrated from countryside to the big city, drawn by the promise of an easier living. The community thrived. Many worked for the Company, with others enlisting in the military where several achieved high ranks and were awarded decorations for bravery. Others worked in construction or the bustling shipyards which furnished the trading boom of the British Empire with fleets to house Indian goods. The oil pressing tradition died out, eventually, as other players had already captured that particular market.

Their first synagogue, Sha'ar haRahamim, was founded in the city in 1796 by Commandant Samuel Ezekiel Divekar. He was something of a hero, being one of the few soldiers to survive captivity as a prisoner of war by the forces of the Sultan of Mysore. During his capture he made himself a promise: if he survived imprisonment, he would build a synagogue for the Bene Israel of Bombay. He had heard of them from his contact with the Jews of Cochin. The war hero was as good as his word.

The synagogue proved to be just the beginning and by 1838, the community had grown to 8,000—more than the Cochini and Baghdadi Jews put together. Eventually in 1875 a Hebrew-Marathi School was established in Bombay known as the Israelite School. As educational establishments such as these flourished, the level of literacy rose among the community and out of its numbers graduated advocates, physicians, engineers, accountants and civil servants. Yet the community was not entrepreneurial on the whole and preferred safe jobs, often in government services.

Relations in India's cosmopolitan melting pot were good with the people of other religions in the city. Each community respected the religious practices of the other. As the community became established it started to use nearby Pune as a summer retreat. Others got jobs that involved them being stationed throughout the Indian empire, so the community branched out to new cities including Ahmedabad, Delhi and as far north as Karachi in modern-day Pakistan. However, these satellite communities were never more than a handful of Jews, and as a result did not register highly on the radar of the ruling Mughal powers of the north, where the dominant Hindus and Sikhs faced merciless persecution at times during this era.

While British rule endured, the educated Bene Israel did well. By the 1940s, the community had reached a peak of 25,000 people in India. The Bene Israel was like the Cochinis in that they also differentiated between fair- and dark-skinned Jews. This color distinction was also mirroring the indigenous society which put a premium on fairness. But the difference with the Bene Israel is their community to this day numbers thousands—evidence in itself of their ability to overcome their divisions in time and survive.

Also like the Cochinis, they too caught the attention of visiting foreigners who recognized them as a distinct people from the other Indians. One European Jewish traveler records his encounter in 1947. "Their garb and their complexion seemed foreign, but their eyes shining like little stars were as unmistakably Jewish as those of our boys in Poland who used to chant the Friday evening prayers with similar enthusiasm," said Henry Shoskes in *Your World and Mine*. He was clearly moved to find these lost Jews in the heart of India.

"Choking with emotion, Cynowicz and I joined in the song. We did not mind the strangeness of the tune, the words or their meaning; the faith they expressed was the same as we have always known."

The axis of events of 1947 and 1948—Indian Independence and the creation of Israel—would usher in irrevocable change, however. The Bene Israel became concerned for their economic prospects under the new political order in India as many had relied on the old British raj for their survival. Therefore, the combined lure of Zionism and new opportunities in Israel led many to leave forever.

* * * *

The raj proved pivotal in the fortunes of all the Jews of India. The rise of Bombay under the British led to Cochin's eventual demise as the premier trading port of the west coast, which in turn impacted on the fortunes of the Jews there. In Bombay itself, the transformation taking place as a result of British trading led to the Bene Israel people migrating from village to city and tying their fortunes with the raj. In the case of the Baghdadi Jews of Bombay and Calcutta, they came to India from the

Persian Gulf port of Basra which was another outpost of the British Empire around 1760. At this point, Jews involved in trade with India arrived from Basra and Baghdad, at first settling on the western coast of India. A community of one hundred Jews came from this part of the world to Surat, forming an Arabic speaking Jewish colony. These merchants were named Baghdadi or Iraqi Jews and in time others from Syria, Persia and Afghanistan joined them. Surat declined, leading important Jewish families such as the Sassoons, Abrahams, Ezras and Kadouries to move towards the new British-ruled commercial hubs of Bombay and Calcutta. Fortunes were made through trade in cotton, jute, tobacco and opium.

Within a century of their move to India the Arabic-speaking Jewish community numbered almost thirty families and the center of their religious life was a house rented from Parsis, who hailed originally from Persia. Thus, the old world and new conspired to survive.

The most famous of the Baghdadi Jews, whose name resonates in India to this day, is David Sassoon. He arrived in Bombay in 1833, the ancestor of the chief treasurer to the governor of Baghdad. He forged his own legacy in India as the head of a trading dynasty which would eventually stretch from Calcutta and Bombay to Shanghai and Singapore. He also became a renowned philanthropist which together with his commercial pedigree earned him the appellation of "the Rothschild of the East."

Among his charitable activities was the building of the Magen David synagogue in Bombay in 1861, which included a religious school and hostel. Thanks to his company, Jews from across India found jobs in the Sassoon factories in Bombay. His corporate ethos was based on patrician values: he took it upon himself to provide food and accommodation for

Jews arriving in the city, as well as arranging medical care and schooling for the children. The schools even taught ritual slaughter to ensure that families who were posted to remote areas far from other Jews could maintain their religious practices.

Sassoon's contribution to Bombay life was acknowledged beyond his own people. On his death in 1864, the *Times of India* wrote that "Bombay has lost one of its most energetic, wealthy, public spirited and benevolent citizens ..."

His successors continued his work of building a textile empire and also endowed charities, schools and built cemeteries for the Baghdadi Jews of Bombay. The second largest group of Baghdadi Jews settled in Calcutta, which was India's eastern trading port. Many were Iraqis who had fled the tyranny of the Daud Pasha (1817–1831). The founding father of this branch of the Baghdadi Jews was Moses Dwek ha Cohen who served as head of the community, honorary rabbi and *mohel*, according to *The Jews of India*.

They earned their living by becoming merchants in the lucrative trading of opium, silk, indigo and jute and by the nineteenth century had grown to some 1,800 people. A few worked in finance or become landowners. The Ezra and Elias families were dominant players here, like Sassoon, leading the way in employment creation as well as charitable activities.

I.A. Isaac described how the Ezras were drug barons of their day, exporting opium from Calcutta to South East Asia. David Joseph Ezra exported opium to Hong Kong, as well as dealing in more innocuous cargo. He acted as the agent for Arabian ships arriving at Calcutta to offload dates and other produce from Muscat and Zanzibar. Opium was merely one of many revenue earners in his commercial portfolio.

While the Baghdadi Jews were unsentimental in business, they were diligent in matters of religion. These same families helped build a series of synagogues, starting with the Neveh Shalom in 1831. In both cities, the Baghdadi Jews maintained their Iraqi Jewish traditions, as well as Arabic as their first language. They were well regarded by the British rulers and many were named honorary magistrates.

One unfortunate side effect of this closeness to the British was a negative attitude by the paler Baghdadis towards the indigenous Indians: "The Baghdadis wished to assimilate into British society and be considered European," according to *The Jews of India*. As a result they aped European dress and lifestyle, as well as prejudices. The wealthier ones spoke English, not Hindi, Bengali and Marathi, the local Indian languages. They sought to join the stuffy and elitist English clubs—a bizarre little world of afternoon tea and dainty sandwiches, with cricket on the lawns followed by cocktails on the terrace: an Anglicized haven where the Brits could convene in private, away from the riff-raff natives.

The Baghdadis taste for social stratification extended to their fellow Jews. While Cochin's White or Paradesi Jews were warmly accepted by them, the darker skinned Malabari and Bene Israel Jews were not. It mirrored the attitudes of the Paradesis in Cochin who also sought to play up their fairness, Jewish purity and European savoir-faire in order to court the approval of the ruling elite.

For the Baghdadis, this affiliation to the old raj spelled doom when the sun finally set on the Empire in India. As a result, after Indian Independence in 1947, the Baghdadi Jews found their position uncertain. The Socialist inspired government of the new India ushered in import and foreign exchange controls which hit the Jews' business hard. The formation of Israel in 1948 also gave birth to an era of Arab-Israeli tensions in the Middle East, which further impeded the trading opportunities of the Baghdadis. For example, the key markets of Iraq and Egypt were both closed to their trading activities. By the 1940s, the once-invincible Sassoon family closed its factory gates, making thousands of Jews unemployed. By 1973, the mills of the Elias family in Calcutta had also shut down.

The result was economic misery followed by exodus, with many going to Israel or to the West to start over. By the mid 1990s, a community that was 5,000 strong in its heyday had collapsed to less than 200, a decline as precipitous as the Cochinis. Yet unlike their South Indian co-religionists, the Baghdadis never preserved in tact their identity once they moved overseas. It seems the Baghdadis at least, are in this sense, a lost tribe for sure.

* * * *

CHAPTER SEVEN

Son of Salem

"Courage has never been known to be a matter of muscle; it is a matter of the heart. The toughest muscle has been known to tremble before an imaginary fear. It was the heart that set the muscle trembling."

—GANDHI, 1931

E very town has its maverick. In Mattancherry's Jew Town that man was Gamy Salem: self-confessed cynic, scourge of convention and one who viewed the Cochini Jews' checkered history with an unsparingly critical eye. He came from one of the Cochini Jewry's most distinguished dynasties, a family of iconoclasts. His father had been known as the "Jewish Gandhi."

The elder Salem had five children: two daughters and three sons. The sons, Raymond, Balfour and Gamy, all inherited the Salem spirit, but only Gamy survives still. In the 1950s, Gamy's brother Balfour defied the conservative White elders by marrying Baby Koder, daughter of a prominent White Jewish family. It was the first intermarriage and blew apart the old dividing line. In a way, he was continuing his father's work of breaking down barriers. Where A.B. Salem had used the law and non-violent protests like his mentor Gandhi, his son Balfour changed local history by standing by his love for Baby.

Gamy also followed his brother in marrying a White Jewess, Reema, although things were much easier by the time their turn came. Sitting in his front parlor on Synagogue Lane, we would speak for hours on end. I came to enjoy our afternoon interludes over glasses of fizzy Mirinda and snacks. "Jew Town's sole skeptic" as he called himself was a welcome relief from the prickliness of some of his neighbors. His approach to life was not bound by the strictures of orthodoxy and status. One sensed that for Gamy the world held deeper pleasures, more sparkling sensations than those of the synagogue and tradition. Here was an old man with a taste for trouble and an appetite for wider possibilities in life, even now, in his eighth decade.

When it came to his community, he feigned indifference, even amusement at this narrow little world, yet clearly he was deeply bound to it—despite his best efforts to disguise the fact that he cared. He remained one of the few willing to confront the past and future honestly. As one of the Black Jews in Ernakulam put it, "Gamy's the only fellow over there who's not a damned fool."

Indeed, he was no fool, although sometimes he liked to play one. He was funny and kind with it. Strangers were drawn to his door by the tantalizing delights of easy conversation, bad jokes, worse whisky and fizzy drinks that glowed like radioactive waste. Seeing me stalking Synagogue Lane day in, day out, amused him. He would watch me from his doorway, feign horror, pretend to hide and then tease: "Your Enemy Number One (Sammy Hallegua) has gone to the market. I can talk for two minutes, *then* I have an urgent appointment to play bridge with my old ladies in Fort Cochin." He wasn't kidding about timing conversations. If he said he'd give you two minutes and gave you fifteen, next time you came by, he'd tell you that you were already in debt with him and he would not extend any more credit. I couldn't help liking him and his wife.

A handsome man with the darker complexion more common to Keralites than the almost translucent fairness of the White Jews, he had a head of steel grey hair, and sported the local dress of short sleeved shirt hanging loosely over a white cotton checked *lunghi* tied at the waist. Reema was still a great beauty, with a flawless milky complexion, smooth forehead and the clear bright eyes of woman years younger. Together, they were a striking couple. So opposite in looks and temperament, yet like all really happy couples, when together they were seamless. They seemed to be relatively untouched by the melancholy that permeated the neighborhood, although there were times when they too succumbed.

Their home was simple, with a long corridor-style living room that opened straight onto the street through shuttered doors. Through to the right was another room, a dining area, with table and chairs, a fridge and walls adorned with huge framed family photos, including one of A.B. Salem. Black and white stills of the Jews in their heyday, dressed up and partying as well as shiny, bright snaps of grandchildren. Their Christian servant Mary, a diminutive old lady standing at four feet ten inches and dressed in a floral *kaftan*, would hover in and out of the living room as she went about her chores. She had just had her cataracts removed, paid for by her master. Rather incongruously, she wore glamorous Jackie Onassis style dark glasses that engulfed her tiny features as she polished and tidied and went about her work. Now and then she would come over to us and stand with one leg cocked coquettishly behind her, as she listened with her head to the side, even though her English was minimal. Her ease echoed that of her employers, for this was a happy house. And the master was never happier then when playing mischief. It was his chief pastime on a street where little happened anymore. He had a keen eye for comedy and would gather scurrilous scraps of gossip and feed these tidbits to his wife and friends. Nothing was sacred or exempt from his humor, not even the synagogue. Pomposity, greed, vanity were favorite targets.

One afternoon, as I took my habitual rest in his front room, a couple of visitors going to Sarah's house caught Gamy's attention. The unwitting prey for his caustic wit was a father and his sixteen-year-old son. They were converted Christians from Chennai, from across the state line in Tamil Nadu. Gamy began to tell me their story, his right hand occasionally lifting to his mouth as if to suppress a guffaw.

"See these two here. I call them Fool Number One and Fool Number Two. They're low caste Hindus who converted to Christianity. Why? They were poor people and they thought it would bring a better life. Only thing, nobody got rich from going to Church. They hear about the White Jews. Old people, big houses and no children. Understand?"

I looked at this poor couple, wreathed in sweat as they struggled down the street with numerous heavy bags of food shopping, and felt an instinctive dread about their story.

"They come to Jew Town, they meet Sarah. They become friends. Our Sarah's no fool, unlike our visitors from Chennai," he sniggers, then sucks his teeth back in. "She tells them she cannot get quality vegetables in Cochin market, that the food is better in Chennai. So, every two weeks our friends come by train across the mountains, carrying heavy bags of Sarah's favorite fruit and vegetables. From Chennai. For free!"

"Are these foods only available in Chennai?"

"*Same* food as from here. These are poor people, they cannot afford. Yet they bring free food. And Sarah lets them do it."

"If they can't afford it, why do it?"

"They believe when Sarah dies, they'll inherit her house. Everyone knows about Jew Town. So, the vultures fly across the mountains of Kerala, fly in from the villages and towns, to come and wait for their chance. The young Muslim boys who sell postcards outside her house. You know them?"

"Yes."

"Same story." He wobbled his head in affirmation.

"Has she promised the Chennai people the house?"

"Sarah's already made provisions for her will. These fellows won't get it. Her young Muslim boys won't get it. But Sarah's smart. While she lives, everyone is dancing to her tune."

The real estate on Synagogue Lane was expensive. This was one of the most important tourist destinations in Kerala, attracting caravans of visitors every day from across India. But more importantly it was a place that drew rich foreigners, not just of Jewish origin, but of every background. For that reason, everyone wanted a piece of Jew Town. It was a point that was not lost on any of the Paradesis. This was also part of their defensiveness: the fear that people were waiting, quite literally, to slide into their slippers.

Gamy told me the Chennai family was so keen to win Sarah's favor that they were planning to convert once again—this time to Judaism. On the last visit, the father had informed Gamy he planned to have his teenage son circumcised. I was about to hear the story for myself as the Chennai couple popped in to see old uncle Gamy. The father, a small and immaculately turned out man in his forties, gingerly hovered on the threshold. His tall, shy son stood awkwardly behind him with a look of suffering on his face that seemed out of place.

Gamy nodded towards the doorway, then turned to me and said, *sotto voce*: "Here he comes, Circumcision Boy."

"Uncleji. I've brought my son to see you. We've just seen Aunty and she is well."

"Come, come," said Gamy, the generous host. He made his introductions to me and offered them a seat on the sofa but they insisted on standing, in an uncomfortable, deferential mode in front of Gamy's planter's chair. They may have left Hinduism behind for Christianity and now Judaism, but the old caste mentality was harder to relinquish.

"Uncleji," the father began hesitantly, eyes lowered and palms in *namaste*, "We have some good news." He gently pushed his son forward towards Gamy.

"My boy has had the great honor of being circumcised," he announced proudly.

Gamy paused at this momentous pronouncement, took in a sharp breath and then turned to the boy, clasping his hands in congratulations.

"Ah, but this is terrific news. And, tell me, *where* did they do it?"

There was a long pause.

"Chennai," said the boy in a strangled voice. "Two days ago."

I offered my congratulations to him as he blushed terribly. It was traumatic enough to be circumcised at sixteen, without being dragged across two states to deliver vegetables to a wily old lady in Cochin and then have his most intimate news conveyed to the whole town. All this and he was still technically a Christian.

"Did it hurt, Baba?"

"Uncleji, it was *very* painful," the boy confirmed, head wobbling in agitation as he twisted his legs from one side to the other, either in embarrassment or pain or both.

"You've done a great thing," said Gamy. "Many congratulations."

With that, the father and son clasped Gamy's hands once more and gazed into his eyes with gratitude, murmuring thanks. Their action had met with approval. The boy then touched the old man's feet in the traditional act of deference and they announced they were on their way home, all the way back to Tamil Nadu. As they headed off towards the bus-stop, Gamy turned to me and said archly, "*Now* you are knowing why I'm calling them Fools Number One and Two."

* * * *

Synagogue Lane was in the throes of the festivals. It had commemorated the Day of Atonement, a day for reflection, remorse and prayer for renewal. It had celebrated Sukkoth, the feast of the Tabernacles which remembered the ancient Jews' time in the desert.

Now they were preparing for two of the most joyous celebrations: Shmini and Simhat Torah. It had taken a whole week to prepare the synagogue and the feasts that would accompany the occasion. Today, although Sammy and the community still carefully observed all the proper preparations and customs, there was none of the thrilling anticipation that marked the old days.

As I sat in a café just moments from their street I pondered their old life. Images of the festivals of previous generations, with the men dressed in their best suits, the ladies in their finest embroidered *saris*, jewels twinkling at their white throats and ears; impish children, blushes of pink in fat cheeks, black curls dancing at their temples as they tore up and down Synagogue Lane, sticky pockets crammed with festival sweets.

Festival was nothing without the food. I would taste a real Cochini Jewish banquet in my time here and it was some of the best food I have ever had. I remember an Indian friend telling me once, "Food reflects its people. Bland food makes for bland human beings."

The Cochini Jews' food was a fusion not just of Israel and India, but the rest of the world; its plate was a map of the world. These people had come from Israel, across the Middle East, from Portugal, Spain, Germany and other places over the centuries. When one tasted the table of the Cochini Jews, it was a sensory reminder that this was a migratory people who had been banished, found asylum in disparate lands and absorbed the best they had to offer. Their food was infused with the traces of all these adoptive cultures, while remaining very much Jewish in terms of which foods were eaten, how it was prepared and of course the symbolism that accompanied the simplest acts such as the breaking of bread. Wherever they traveled to, wherever they found sanctuary, the Jews carried their history in their recipes, each dish an evocation of exile, a tribute to their homeland.

I drank down my milkshake, paid the bill and came knocking at Gamy's door, part of my daily ritual. He greeted me warmly and then after scanning the Hallegua house to ensure the warden was not around, he invited me in. Reema was out and Gamy was in the middle of an important business transaction. The fish wallah had just arrived on his bicycle with the day's catch. The two were locked in negotiations over the contents of the wicker basket, which was covered with a wet muslin cloth to keep the fish fresh. Gamy lifted the cloth, peered and prodded at the bounty within. Ali the Muslim fishmonger talked through the catch as though discussing the merits of uncut diamonds. Once the choice was made, he took the fish through to Gamy's kitchen at the back and collected payment.

He warmly wished Gamy goodbye and then mounted his bike again, letting out his plaintive cry to the neighborhood that the fish was in. Gamy went to re-examine his purchase, evidently delighted. For a South Indian, there are few sights more uplifting than a fat, wet fish. He lifted the plate to examine it more closely. I asked him if the fish was for the festival, but he said this was nothing special, unlike the sea-bass that Babu had purchased. Word had spread to Mattancherry of the Ernakulam Jews' good fortune. I sensed a tinge of envy as Gamy commented, "I hear he paid over 1,000 rupees. I doubt it will be worth the price."

The thought of glistening seabass at festival time summoned up the memory of tables laden for past celebrations. "We used to have such a *pukka* Jewish life," Gamy sighed. "We used to celebrate like *hell!*" Yet when the others left for Israel, Gamy and Reema stayed.

"Israel's in our prayers. Of course, it is. It's something like our religious duty. But I'm very happy I didn't go to live there. I've been there four or five times. Not bad! But we have a better life here. Why lose that?"

His hand gestured to the street in ample explanation, to the palms, to the sea, to the ease of having a fishmonger come to your door, whom you could exchange pleasantries with and allow into your kitchen to wash your fish and cool it in a dish of water. Small things like this made it hard to leave. Only a minority felt this way. Not even his own children felt this way about India and all the good things it had given the Jews: land, security, peace. His children had gone in search of jobs and partners overseas.

"There weren't any prospects for marriage here then, to allow them to stay?"

"Have you *met* any young people here? Have you even *seen?*" he said, his face a mask of incredulity. "You know who they are. Yaheh is here. Keith is here. Stay or go. He doesn't know what to do. He wanted to get married, long ago. Yaheh's sister he would have married. When he couldn't have her, he didn't want the other. End of story." That simple sentence pretty much said it all.

"I told you, everybody is waiting for the end now," he sighed as he rose from his favorite spot to fetch some more water. He returned bearing two glasses of iced *panni*, placing them by our chairs. He sipped lightly from his glass, eyes closing as he winced at the coldness of the water. "Now, if I die tomorrow, these people," he pointed to the postcard hawkers who were now eavesdropping outside his doorway, "Muslims will have to carry me to my grave. Because there are not enough of our own men. Our dead, they never used to *touched* by outsiders. Now there's no option."

Outside it turned dark as the clouds heralded another storm ahead. Gamy went to turn on the single low-wattage light bulb in the living room but the electricity had cut out, which was typical enough. He slumped back into his chair as if exhausted by the effort, chin dipped into his chest, and resumed where he had left off. He had a theory as to why things had panned out this way, he told me. The Jews had once been lucky, he said. "They caught the right people." In the same way a wise fisherman knew where he could most profitably cast his net. "We caught people who could help us, like the raja. We were canny that way." Whereas Jews elsewhere in the world suffered at the hands of others, the Cochini Jewry could not blame outsiders for what had happened. They were given the most perfect set of circumstances and still things got spoiled.

The history of prejudice against the Blacks by the Whites had jinxed them, he said. It was the old Jewish belief of the link between justice and *shalom*. "There is some curse in this town," he said softly, with all the melodrama that only a Jewish Indian can muster. His eyes shone, long yellowed teeth protruding slightly as he warmed to his unsettling theme. "Nobody will ever rise above average. It's true!" he insisted, now sitting forward in his chair.

"So many of us were smart. Brilliant, even. Brilliant minds from rich families, high connections, a great history. But where has it got us? To the edge of extinction. Is it our curse?

"We had eight synagogues, the Blacks and Whites, a history that went back to the great age of Solomon. Now there's one synagogue here, two are empty in Ernakulam. And the rest? Vanished or crumbling into ruins, homes to snakes and rats. We're just fifty where there were once thousands."

He went quiet again, jutting his jaw out as he scratched the bristly grey stubble on his chin. Clearly, for all the jokes, it troubled him deeply. Gamy saw a collective malaise had descended on the White Jews in particular—this much was evident. It was a recurring theme in the faded salons of Synagogue Lane. Talk of curse, of retribution, each yet another incarnation of an intolerable guilt that pressed down upon the nape of their necks like cold stone. Most were old. Those who were not old were depressed, sick, reclusive or unmarried. The rest were buried in the grave-yard just a few hundred yards away, a walled cemetery with the gate bolted and padlocked to keep out tourists and drunks who came there at night to lie on the gravestones and drink toddy. After several nocturnal episodes of drunken carousing and reports of urination on the tomb-stones, the Jews decided to keep the cemetery permanently locked. It had come to this: even their final resting place was the subject of irreverence and defilement.

Gamy rubbed his hand across his face; his eyes were weary and as bloodshot as Yaheh's hound. He needed to rest but he staved off sleep's entreaties. His promise of only five minutes of talking was forsaken as he desired to talk and talk, as if the mere act of expression would expel thoughts that had corrupted his mind over time.

"You know, you mustn't blame Sammy for not speaking of this," he said gently.

"I don't. I can see why he's like this."

"He's not a bad man. He's a good man who carries a burden. Our history, the source of our curse. Look at the fate of Jew Town. Are we *not* being punished by God?" He looked at me intently, the expression on his face giving the answer. "Young people have had to leave to escape its curse. All the children have gone. If they stay what do they have? No scope here, no future, no marriage partners. What's this, if not a curse?"

"Why a curse still? Your own father ended the divide. It's over."

"Yes. My father did his best to stop it. But he was too late to save us."

His father was a subject he rarely discussed, even with the other Co-chinis. In the past, he had resisted having this conversation but now he relented. I was to discover it was not easy being the son of Salem. Salem's was an awesome legacy, one which should have inspired pride in all Jews. Black and White. As other Indians fought the great political battle of the time, for Independence from the British, Salem also fought for freedom. But his battle was at home, in his own street, at his synagogue.

Abraham Barak Salem was born into a poor family in 1882 but rose from his modest background to become the first graduate among his people. Armed with his degree in law, he shunned the chance to become a politician of national stature to focus on local issues instead. He was a natural populist, fighting the causes of the ordinary man, the underdog. He would launch his public addresses from a hillside in Ernakulum, which become dubbed "Salem Hill" in tribute to this fiery orator. It became a kind of Speaker's Corner, yet devoted to the passionate monologues of just one man who would extol his anger from a hilltop, advocating his case to the treetops, issuing his demand for justice to the clouds.

In the end, people heeded him. And Cochin would remember him. In Jew Town today, one of the approach roads to the synagogue is called A.B. Salem Road, the same synagogue that he was once barred from entering.

After the creation of Israel, A.B. Salem was also tasked with going to the new motherland to plead the case of Malabari Jews wishing to emigrate there. At first, there were some obstacles to their migration because of incidents of elephantiasis among the Cochin Jews. Elephantiasis is an insect-borne disease which causes the head or limbs to swell to huge proportions. A.B. Salem went to Israel to explain that this was not a condition that could be spread and therefore was no danger to the fledgling nation. After his special pleading, the Israeli authorities relented and the ban was relaxed. Ironically, his success marked the beginning of the end for the community and the way of life that he strived so hard to safeguard.

But his greatest success was fighting for the religious equality of the Black Jews. Taking his cue from Gandhi's non-violent form of protest in the fight for Indian Independence, he applied similar tactics to the Paradesi community. By the late 1940s he had succeeded in winning certain rights for his people. Gandhi's methods would eventually spread beyond India, inspiring Martin Luther King, Jr., during the American civil rights movement as well as shaping Nelson Mandela's own political philosophy in South Africa to bridge the divide between Black and White. In Jew Town, the achievements of its own local hero were not universally acknowledged. Admission of Salem's legacy was inevitably an admission of guilt for some of the Whites.

Even in Salem's old house, in his own son, one sensed there were conflicting feelings when discussing those days. For Gamy, it awakened emotions I had never expected: reticence, but more surprisingly, a disappointment and even bitterness. His father was a great man. But Gamy felt he could have been greater had he lifted his eyes beyond the small town feud of the Cochini Jews to the bigger picture of the Indian Independence movement that was sweeping across India in Salem's heyday. Gamy told me that greatness had called at his father's door. But Salem was out. At the synagogue.

A talented young Jewish lawyer, Salem attracted the attention of India's most glittering political son, Jawaharlal Nehru. He was invited by Nehru to participate in a key national Congress meeting. It could have been the political break of a lifetime, catapulting him into national consciousness, but his father in the end chose the synagogue.

"He should have been a great man, but he ended up being a very small man. You know, he had the potential to be a senior leader at national level, given his intellect and contacts. To know Nehru and Gandhi personally, to be a distinguished lawyer, to be one of the brightest of his generation."

It had not been an easy journey. He came from the poor community of the Ernakulam Black Jews. To attend the Madras law college he had to undertake a journey of boat, bullock cart and then train to Madras. He was the first in his community to graduate and once his youngest son Gamy was born, he moved the family to Mattancherry where they remained.

Gamy felt his father wasted his talents on Jew Town, which did not deserve him. Yet without A.B. Salem, equality would have taken longer. Salem had fought and won important causes for his people, he had raised children who went on to become doctors, engineers, lawyers. He had the respect of most of the community, even now. What was this, if not greatness? Yet Gamy remained unconvinced. Equality came to Cochin, but it arrived too late. His father had squandered talent and ambition on a cause that was doomed to failure.

"If he stuck to politics he could have been a great man, but he preferred the synagogue, the Jewish community, the festivals. He was obsessed with local issues. He had a looking glass, 'Salem's Looking Glass' we called it, where he pasted newspaper clippings, ideas, issues that caught his interest. He would take these issues and fight for them, go to his hillside and speak for hours to ordinary people who came and listened. His aim in life was to bring up the poor people, but at the same time he brought himself down."

In India, politics is the route to not just lofty purpose, but also personal enrichment and aggrandizement. In an arena awash with dirty ambition, Salem had remained true to the values of his faith, to the importance of justice in the community.

I felt Gamy was being tough on his father, but as he himself recognized, perhaps this was because he felt he also failed to live up to his potential. Gamy had always dreamed of getting out, escaping, shaking off Jew Town's strictures to explore a world that sang to his adventurous soul. He had the chance and he blew it. He could not forgive himself. Nor could he forgive his father, whose chances had been even greater.

"I find fault with my father, I find fault with myself," he told me, in confessional mood that stormy afternoon just before the onset of Shabbat. "I went to the U.S., studied on a scholarship at Cornell, but came back here, got stuck, ended in same position. Same thing. Same fate. So who am I to criticize? But I did not have my father's talent. I'm just an average person compared to him."

"Aren't you proud of your father's efforts?"

"Of course I'm proud. But I would've been prouder if he'd answered the calls to greater things that kept knocking at his door. He ignored those calls."

Despite choosing this path and renouncing the lure of national politics, Salem retained close relations with the Nehru dynasty which brought the Kerala Jews to prominent attention, once again enabling the community to punch above its weight for a little while longer. Gamy said one such example was when Nehru accompanied his daughter Indira

Gandhi to visit the synagogue. The synagogue was even immortalized on an Indian stamp one year. Jew Town was a valuable symbol of India's secular ideal, demonstrating its tradition of religious tolerance that stretched way back.

Down the timeline of Cochini Jewish history, there are moments that resonate through the millennia: the first contact with the kingdom of Solomon; the fall of the Second Temple; the arrival of Joseph Rabban on Indian shores; the loss of Cranganore and the arrival of the Jews from Europe who would initiate the divide between Black and White. In the late nineteenth century, the powerful advocacy of a Black Jew would restore Judaism's ancient tradition of imparting justice. It was a legacy that was not his alone. Salem built upon the work of those before him, including his own grandfather, as well as unknown Jews, faceless heroes who fought for centuries to break the color bar of Jew Town. This was Cochin's civil rights movement. Except, it started in the sixteenth century and did not conclude until America's own campaign for equality was at its height in the 1950s and 1960s. The fight began where it ended in Salem's time: in the Paradesi Synagogue, which was the focal point in the quest for equality.

* * * *

CHAPTER EIGHT

Segregation in the Synagogue

"You must not be guilty of unjust verdicts . . .
You must not slander your own people . . .
You must not bear hatred for your brother in your own heart . . .
If a stranger lives with you in your land, do not molest him . . .
You must count him as one of your countrymen and love him as
yourself—for you yourselves were once strangers in Egypt."

—LEVITICUS 19:1-2, 11-18

After the loss of the Second Temple, the Jewish people were bereft. At first, they believed they had been abandoned by God. In the past the Temple represented the divine presence amongst them and as such it was the focal point of faith. Its destruction for a second time led the Jews to believe that it was wrong to cherish ambitions to resurrect the Temple a third time. After all, it was not Yahweh's wish.

Instead they would find a new way to worship and in the end substitute the synagogue for the Temple in their day-to-day prayers: so the synagogue came to represent the lost Temple, a physical manifestation of faith at the centre of every Jewish community around the world. Its very structure emulated the hierarchy of the sacred chambers in the old

Temple. The holy of holies, where Yahweh once resided, was evoked in the synagogue by the Ark which contained the Torah scrolls or Law of Judaism.

Shabbat was celebrated here, providing a new setting for the Jews to commune directly with the divine. The *Shekinah* or divine presence manifested itself wherever a *minyan* was formed. Through prayer they could welcome Yahweh in their midst again, wherever they may be, scattered as they were across the continents.

In this way the synagogue became the continuum of the Temple. Although it could never be supplanted in the Jewish heart, the synagogue was the nearest the people had to a link with God. Knowing this, one begins to appreciate the measure of anguish the Black Jews felt when they were told they were not equal before God in the synagogue. It was a rejection that struck at their very core.

* * * *

Rabbi ibn Zimra's edict in 1520 marked the first tentative step in the arduous journey to equality that would take four centuries to travel. The Rabbi backed the Black Jews in their campaign, saying they did indeed have the right to intermarry and enter the synagogue as equals, provided all the proper conversion rituals had taken place. But the Paradesi leaders refused to budge and ignored the foreign Rabbi's rulings.

A generation later, the Black Jews resurrected their campaign in another letter which was dispatched to a former student of ibn Zimra, Rabbi Jacob de Castro in Alexandria. After studying his teacher's earlier missives, he reiterated that equality and marriage between the two groups were permissible. But again, the Paradesi Jews got round the situation by simply filing the letter into oblivion.

On the face of it, discrimination was targeted at the so-called *meshuchrarim*, or "manumitted ones", referring to former slaves who were freed by their Jewish masters. In reality, though, the slave tag was used by the Whites to refer to anyone in the synagogue community they deemed to be non-white. The slur of slavery continued long after the British abolished the practice.

The Paradesis introduced a law that said their congregation did not recognize as equals children born from unions between white men and non-white women. A 1757 entry in the Record Book of the Paradesi Synagogue (page 82–83, according to Katz and Goldberg) sets the position out clearly: "If an Israelite or Ger (convert) marries a woman from the daughters of the Black Jews or the daughters of the meshuchrarim (manumitted slaves), the sons born to them go after the mother; but the man, the Israelite or Ger, he stands in the congregation of our community and he has no blemish."

During these centuries, there were eight synagogues across Cochin, seven of which were used by the Black Jews. But the eighth synagogue, the Paradesi, was a bastion of white purity. Any Black Jews who lived in its proximity faced a ferocious battle for access. The Blacks were denied entry to the synagogue, denied the right to perform rituals there, banned from chanting certain liturgical hymns, banned from reading the Torah or scriptures, and prohibited from marrying into White Jewish families. All the above were seen as polluting acts which could taint the purity of the Paradesi community. Black families were barred from burying their dead in coffins or in the Paradesi Synagogue cemetery a few hundred meters away. In worship, love and even death, the color of a Jew's skin determined his destiny. All these acts directly flouted Jewish law.

The Black Jews took on the discrimination one issue at a time. But the seminal battle was for equality in faith. For four hundred years, Mattancherry's Black Jews were not allowed to sit on the benches of the Paradesi synagogue. Instead, they were relegated to sitting on the dirt floor of the anteroom outside the synagogue itself. From this lowly position they could hear services conducted by the White community. It was shocking to foreign observers even then.

Claudius Buchanan, a missionary who visited Cochin between 1806 and 1808 wrote, "It is only necessary to look at the countenance of the Black Jews to be satisfied that their ancestors must have arrived in India many ages before the White Jews." He then added that despite this lineage, "The White Jews look upon the Black Jews as an inferior race and as not of a pure caste."

A modern-day observer, Rabbi Louis Rabinowitz, said in his writings in *Far East Mission* that the situation in Cochin was comparable to apartheid-era South Africa, where "irrational prejudices take precedence over law and logic and ethics."

He noted parallels with South African apartheid in that whites were the dominant section of society even though they were a minority—representing one third of the local congregation in Mattancherry. If ever the segregation was challenged by the Blacks, the Whites would call upon the raja or local colonial powers to intervene on their behalf and quell any resistance.

The Blacks tried hard to resist and challenge the discrimination in the synagogue. Katz and Goldberg said a number of visiting foreign Jews also lobbied on the Blacks' behalf for equality, but to no avail. By 1840, the Blacks found their situation to be intolerable and relations had reached a point where something had to give. Either the Whites must end the discrimination or the Blacks would rebel. In the end, it was rebellion.

The Blacks escalated the pressure, leading to the protestors being ejected from the synagogue community. Barred from worship even in the Paradesi synagogue anteroom, some of the Black Jews asked for permission to establish their own place of worship in one of the homes in Jew Town. The White leaders refused even this compromise. Following one particularly acrimonious exchange, the Whites enlisted the support of the local *Diwan*, who decreed that no prayer services be conducted by "the group with impurity in the house appropriated for that purpose" according to Johnson's "Our Community in Two Worlds". In a further insult, the Blacks were instructed by the *Diwan* to "walk submissively" to the White Jews, by way of contrition.

The "group with impurity" was led by a Black Jew called Avraham or Avo Hallegua, the grandfather of A.B. Salem. Who was Avo? One version of his history says that he was the son of a rich landowner Shlomo Hallegua and a woman named Hannah who was either born a slave or was the descendant of a poor foreign Jewish family. Either way, Hannah's Jewish credentials were deemed dubious and not acceptable to the white community. Therefore, the marriage of Shlomo Hallegua and Hannah was not conducted in the synagogue but took place at his grand estate in Vettacka.

They conceived a son and Avo was born and grew up on the Hallegua estate. During this time, according to a document of manumission, Hannah was freed on the eve of Passover in 1826, with a stipulation that her sons be counted in the *minyan*. This act should have cleansed her of the past and accorded her offspring full rights in the synagogue. After this key event, Avo was given a full Jewish education and schooled in the teachings of the Torah.

But even a wealthy landowner like Hallegua was not impervious to the pressure of his peers. He was urged to marry a white woman. He did so and she also bore a son. When Hallagua died, Avo took over the estate and managed the business single-handed as his half brother was still a child. But once the child reached adulthood, the old order re-asserted itself.

The younger brother, a White Jew, barred his brother from the an-cestral estate and took his share of the inheritance. The Paradesis rallied to the younger brother's side as the dispute became evermore steeped in bitterness. In the end, the matter was taken before the Cochini raja who ruled in favor of the white brother.

Avo lost everything. He was barred from his home and denied his share in the family estate which he had run since his father died. Overnight, he had become an outcast. Such a brutal rejection would have broken most men. But Avo was unlike others. He channeled the anger over his stolen birthright into a broader campaign: to take on the Pa-radesis directly, not over inheritance or land, but over the religious rights that had been denied to Black Jews like him for centuries. In his view, this was the most unforgivable of all the humiliations suffered by his people. It was the font of all inequality—the idea that the Blacks were somehow lesser Jews than Whites—the poisoned source from which all other in-justices sprang. In this manner, Avo rose from being a disenfranchised landowner to Cochin's first Black Jewish civil rights leader.

After the Blacks were banned from having their own separate synagogue in Mattancherry's Jew Town, a group broke away and resettled in
the British territory of Fort Cochin, a short distance away. There, they
turned a private house into a synagogue and Avo took on the role of religious scribe or *sofer* as well as *shohet*. At first, their new community
proved to be successful. The resettled Black Jews thrived and were integrated into the local community. They got on well with their non-Jewish neighbors and reports of those times showed the Black Jews as
well-to-do. The Jewish women sported gold jewelry and their households
even employed servants. Their revived fortunes contrasted sharply with
their old rivals, the Paradesis, who were by this time considerably less
well off.

But benevolence's blessing on the Black Jews proved to be short-
lived as disaster struck Fort Cochin. A cholera epidemic swept through
their neighborhood and most of their number was wiped out in a matter of days. The devastated few that survived left for Bombay or Calcutta,
where there were other Jewish communities, or returned to Mattancherry's Jew Town.

The Paradesi leaders reveled in the misfortune of those who came
back. They were told that if they wished to return to their old lowly position on the synagogue anteroom floor, they would have to pay a fine
before being rehabilitated. The Whites saw the defection to Fort Cochin
as an act of blasphemy and insurrection. One of the Whites was a man
called Reinman who wrote about the whole sorry affair in "Masa'oth
Shlomo b'Kogin". He was actually fairly sympathetic, unlike some of the
others, yet even he believed the Blacks had courted catastrophe through
their ill-conceived defiance:

> "God punished the sin of the (Blacks) who were disloyal and
> withdrew from the synagogue of the White Jews and dese-
> crated its holiness ... almost all of (them) died with the plague
> and epidemic . . . and many who remained became mad and
> got out of hand. The remainder of the refugees turned to the
> White Jews and paid a fine to the synagogue to accept them as
> before. Avo ... died naked and for want of everything and his
> only son went out of his mind."

That last line on the fate of Avo would have been a heartbreaking epitaph if that had been the end of the matter. But it was not. Avo's true
legacy was that he imbued a spirit of change in his people. That spirit
remained undiminished even with his death.

In 1882, the Black Jews again asked the *Diwan* to permit them to
worship in a private house. They sought the help of David Sassoon, a
Bombay businessman, who wrote to the British Resident on their behalf.
Again the plea failed. Disappointed and rejected, all they could do was
keep going.

News continued to spread to the Jewish community overseas of the
discrimination practiced in Cochin's Jewry. Rabbinical emissaries arrived in India from Jerusalem to resolve the problem. Just as had happened 300 years earlier, the Chief Rabbi of Jerusalem Rabbi Phanizel,
ruled in 1882 that the so-called "slaves" should enjoy full religious privileges provided the special *t'vilah* ceremony was carried out. History
repeated itself as the Paradesis again defied the Rabbi's ruling. It
seemed even the high-most authorities could not force the Whites to
recognize the Blacks' rights.

It would take the grandson and namesake of Avo to force the change. Where rabbis, elders and foreign emissaries failed, a low-born black lawyer from Ernakulam, A.B. Salem, would succeed. What Avo started, his grandson would finish in the following century.

With his birthright stolen, Salem did not have riches at his disposal, nor vast estates or privilege. But he did inherit his grandfather's indomitable spirit and he was fired by the same zeal for justice. He used his law degree to fight the cases of the oppressed, not just for fellow Jews, but the lowest sections of society. For example, through the organization of trade unions, he helped low-paid workers such as the boatman improve their working rights.

His interest in grass-root politics eventually elevated him into the upper echelons of Cochini society, leading him to serve on the Cochin Legislative Assembly. In 1929 he was a delegate of the native Princely States of Cochin and Travancore to the national Congress meeting in Lahore where Gandhi launched his struggle for independence.

This was a turning point in Cochini Jewish history, as it was for Indian nationalism generally. It was here that Salem was converted to the gospel of Gandhian non-violent protest. He decided that if Indians could fight even the military might of the British using such methods, the Black Jews could deploy this same weapon in their struggle for equality in the synagogue.

Gandhi had used the tactic of passive resistance to successfully campaign on behalf of the Untouchables in neighboring Travancore. The Untouchables, now known as Dalits, were at the bottom of the Hindu caste system, had minimal rights and were ruthlessly exploited by the upper castes. On his return, an inspired Salem organized a *satyagraha* or non-violent resistance in the synagogue. He agreed with Gandhi that religious discrimination was "most pernicious" and was determined to end it in his own backyard.

Just as Gandhi's empowerment through peace ignited the forces of a mass political awakening in India, so the "Jewish Gandhi" also succeeded in his small town revolution. The overturning of a tainted history began with one man staging sit-ins at the synagogue, using his oratory skills to advocate change and even at one stage, threatening to fast until death. Salem recruited his young sons—Raymond, Balfour and Gamy—to the cause, even though they were still small children. He would take his sons to the synagogue and refuse to sit in the designated space for the Blacks on the anteroom floor. Shunning this lowly position, he defiantly strode into the main synagogue itself, dragging his sons behind him.

One man who knew Salem in those heady days of protest was the father of Isaac Joshua, who is the current President of the Association of Kerala Jews and managing trustee of the Ernakulam Synagogue. Isaac, the foremost elder among the Cochini Jews, was now in his mid-eighties, but he had grown up on his father's accounts of the Jewish Gandhi who was a close family friend. "I remember him too well," he said, scratching his shiny copper pate as he summoned up its memories. "He used to come to our house every Saturday and spent Sabbath with us. He was my father's great friend. He came to our house and synagogue for service and then he came for lunch every Saturday.

"Back in those days before the change, the Blacks were forced to sit on the ground outside. Well, Salem wasn't going to take it any longer!" The old man's eyes sparkled as he recalled Salem's audacious plan to enter.

"What happened was he started to sit under the window sill looking into the synagogue. Then *on* the sill. Body was on the sill, but his legs were technically outside. That's how it began. Slowly, he put one leg inside, then the other. These people had no guts to stop him. Then slowly, he came inside and sat there and so it went on. They couldn't stop him," he shook his head as he laughed and wagged his finger. "They couldn't stop this man, they simply looked daggers. He then started taking his sons with him. He was a very strong man and they were scared. He was a top lawyer, a writer, he knew Gandhi, he knew Nehru. Salem was *our* Jewish Gandhi."

Salem did not stop there. He wanted every Jew to have access to the Paradesi Synagogue, the weak as well as the strong. He held full prayer services at his home or joined the prayers at the homes of other Blacks who could withstand the humiliation of the synagogue apartheid no longer. Through such small acts of defiance, Salem effected great change. He skillfully articulated the Black cause, combining his devastating lawyer's logic with a rousing oratory that began to sway younger, more modern thinking members of the Paradesi community. A small number of Whites became convinced that segregation was wrong.

These younger, progressive Whites joined his campaign for change and their support proved to be the vital tipping point which would lead to a revolution on Synagogue Lane. Inspired by Salem, young White Jewish men used their own methods of non-violent protest. They refused to carry the heavy Torah scrolls during the Simhat Torah processions until change was introduced. Their revolt led to a breakthrough—eventually two benches were set up for the Blacks in the back of the Paradesi Synagogue. They were just two small benches at the back of the synagogue. But for the first time in four hundred years, the Black Jews were *inside*. They had moved from the floor of the anteroom to a ringside seat at the heart of religious proceedings. In 1937, the academic and long-time observer of the community Mandelbaum visited and reported an astonishing change: Blacks could read from the Law on weekdays, although not on Sabbath.

Still, Salem was not satisfied. Blessed with formidable patience as well as a ferocious intellect, he relentlessly chipped away at the edifice of prejudice, piece by piece, until it came tumbling down. In 1942, a satisfied Salem recorded in his journal:

> "For the first time in the History of the Paradeshi Synagogue I got the chance, by stressing the law of the religious services regarding the reading of Torah, the privilege of reading the Maphtir of this Sabbath and Rosh Hodesh. May God be praised . . . May the innovation become the order of the day!"

This was the closest the understated Salem got to trumpeting Black Jewish religious emancipation. Yet his exclamation mark at the end of that sentence speaks as clearly as any victory speech of the joy that must have overwhelmed his heart that day. It was just the beginning, as he envisaged. By the close of the decade, there were further landmarks on the road to equality. The Blacks could bury their dead in a separate area of the Paradesi Synagogue cemetery. Blacks and Whites were still not allowed to lie side by side in death, but at least now they could share the same soil. But, most important of all, Black Jews could be called to read Torah on Sabbath and recite blessings.

Yet there was still a way to go. Blacks were barred from holding weddings or circumcisions in the Paradesi synagogue. These had to be conducted at home. Also, marriage between Black and White was still prohibited.

The coming decade would see great change sweeping through Cochin's Jew Town and for Jews worldwide. On the global stage, the world saw the birth of Israel in 1948, which triggered a wave of mass migration of Jews everywhere. The founding fathers of Israel wished to create a rainbow nation, where the Diaspora of every hue and nationality could reunite in their ancient land once more. The idea of Jews of every color coming together to summon up a nation state from the desert sands was a powerful one which, no doubt, inspired further change for the Black and White Jews of Cochin. After all, in the motherland itself every Jew—regardless of color—played an equal part in nation-building.

Within a few years of the creation of Israel and the Blacks winning equality in the Paradesi Synagogue, the last taboo was broken by a passionate affair between two young lovers, Balfour and Baby. Their love is the final chapter in the story of apartheid in Cochin's Jew Town. It took Salem's oldest son and his beautiful and spirited bride to bring the era of segregation to a close. Theirs was a final conflict between love and prejudice. And in keeping with all great romances, prejudice was vanquished. Love won.

* * * *

CHAPTER NINE

Taboo Love

"My dove, your splendor resembles Orion and the Pleiades
And I, for love of you, shall sing a song."
—SIXTEENTH-CENTURY POEM BY ISRAEL MOSES NAJARA,
SUNG BY COCHINI JEWS

W edding fever had gripped Synagogue Lane. A flutter of creamy manila envelopes arrived in the post pronouncing the forthcoming nuptials of the young couple. On hearing the news, for a moment I envisioned some Hollywood-style ending, a sigh-inducing rapprochement in the long running saga of Yaheh and Keith. Had cold indifference graduated to slow burning pragmatism? Had the elders finally bent them into submission or had they decided over too many glasses of "petrol" toddy they would sacrifice themselves to save two thousand years of history after all?

"Don't be a damned fool," said Gamy, as if I'd suggested sun and moon could dance in the same sky. "Balfour and Baby's grandson is getting married in Israel. A nice Jewish girl. Reema, Sammy and Queenie fly out in a few days."

The wedding would be held near Haifa, close to where Baby continued to live after her husband died. There would be no wedding ceremony in Cochin—the last one had taken place generations ago. Still, a wedding was a wedding and if the couple would not come to Cochin, then a banquet would be held in their honor.

The news had the desired effect: the Paradesis walked around with smiles on their faces and it was good to see. A wedding was a time to rejoice and forget the past few weeks, burying Shalom, the stress of organizing the festival season. Forget the difficulties of the past years, indeed. Those attending were in a whirlwind of preparation and those remaining were planning the finest party Jew Town had seen in a while. The couple would be toasted from Israel to India.

"Since your Enemy Number One is flying to Israel," suggested Gamy, "you shall come to the party. Johnny's house, Wednesday, eight o'clock. Just don't tell Sammy."

Sammy, Queenie and Reema would be flying first to Mumbai where they would change flights for Israel. Gamy had already been in touch with Indian Airlines and El Al over the arrangement of wheelchairs to take them through check-in and security. The three of them would need an additional entourage of baggage handlers to deal with the accompanying luggage. I watched in bafflement as Gamy, Reema and old Mary grappled with a dusty brown leather suitcase that had been hauled out of storage for the occasion, and began to pack.

It was the arduous task known to every Indian family, Jewish or not. I had learned from my own family that Indians never travel lightly. The concept of capsule packing is unknown in the subcontinent. Even the shortest of trips required certain essentials: a choice of heirloom jewelry for parties, gifts for the elders, mangos by the box-load, one small bag of superior quality chapatti flour, one kilo each of garam masala, cumin and coriander seeds, chocolate and toys for all the children. And pickle.

Gamy deliberated momentarily over whether the family in Haifa would require dried fish as well, or whether pickle was an adequate condiment option. The packing naturally took days to complete. At one stage, Gamy could be seen throwing small Indian dolls across the parlor floor, raging that he had specifically requested small easy-to-pack toys, not full-size action heroes. The night before departure the brown suitcase sat in the entrance hall, straining at its zipper like a squat Indian gentleman suffering from explosive indigestion after too much butter chicken. For the first time in my life, I pitied the immigration customs officers at Ben Gurion International Airport. They would need a bigger table.

* * * *

Sammy, Queenie, Reema and her suitcase of never-ending treasures departed for Israel. As their white ambassador taxi disappeared from view, Gamy had a look on his face which said, "Let the drinking commence." The men quickly got down to doing what men do best—they carefully judged the amount of whisky that needed to be purchased and consumed that evening. Did the occasion merit just plain Indian whisky or should a bottle of Johnnie Walker Black Label be procured? Such weighty debates went on late into the afternoon. Meanwhile, the women got together, jotted down a menu, shopped and then cooked up a storm under the leadership of Johnny's wife, Juliette, who was widely acknowledged as the best cook on Synagogue Lane.

The party would be held at their house, the Hallegua mansion right at the top of Synagogue Lane. Johnny insisted that as the senior-most elder in Jew Town after Sammy's departure, he would take care of the celebrations. He refused to accept payment or help and Gamy was grateful as it was surely a cost he could ill afford. Everyone was invited. The last Jews of Kerala would gather that evening to celebrate the wedding of the grandson of Baby and Balfour, the first couple to unite the two communities. The only non-attendee was Sarah, who was still in mourning for Shalom. But even she would not miss out on the feast as Juliette had arranged to send her a plate of food. With the solemn presence of the patriarch gone, the mood became light, almost frivolous. Then just before sundown everyone disappeared back into their houses to say evening prayers and get ready.

As I approached the Hallegua mansion that evening, it was unnaturally quiet. I knocked at the door and it opened a crack, just a sliver of light and one eye was visible. It was Yaheh who looked surprised to see me. She had that stern look on her face again.

"Hi, I'm here for the party."

"What party?"

"The wedding party."

"What wedding?"

She was good. She didn't even blink. In a parallel universe she would have been the most *sangfroid* poker player in Vegas. I could imagine her celebrating in the bar after breaking the house, taking to the stage and belting out Bette Midler show tunes.

"Your father and Gamy invited me."

The door closed. A minute passed, then it swung wide open and the doorway suddenly flooded with yellow light, bathing me in conviviality and the distant sound of singing from the back of the house. Yaheh smiled broadly. Not a fake, tight smile, but a real beamer, full of pleasure.

"Come in. You're very welcome in our house. Let me take you through."

She was transformed by the occasion: not just in demeanor but appearance too; she was wearing light makeup, lipstick-mouth like a summer strawberry and dressed in a rainbow silk *kaftan* that rippled color as she moved. She led me through the old house, suddenly effusive with pride and hospitality. The entrance parlor was a grand room with dizzily high ceilings and wonderful mosaic floors made for waltzing. Antique carved furniture adorned the room and a television set buzzed away in the corner as some of the young men from Ernakulam watched the cricket, periodically shrieking their delight. The house was almost three hundred years old and its original character very much unchanged. The cracked plastered walls breathed memories of the past sorrows and celebrations of the White Jews and I wished I could discern their secrets. From the salon we walked through to a long corridor. Seated on a pew alongside one wall were the ladies, all attired in their finest outfits, primped and pretty as if waiting to be asked to dance.

The aunties cooed their welcome as Yaheh introduced me. Most of them, I already knew. The older ladies wore embroidered chiffon *saris* in the colors of Kerala: petrol blue, lime green, dusty pink. Gold bangles jangled on their arms as they carefully smoothed down their dark hair, polished and perfumed with coconut oil. Dangling earrings swung from their ears as their heads turned from side to side in conversation and many wore the traditional Jewish wedding necklace. There were just a couple of young girls from Ernakulam, shy and awkward, in trendy

Westernized clothes, sipping cola and squirming with displeasure as their mothers fussed over them. Juliette and Yaheh ran the proceedings with effortless aplomb, keeping the conversation, food and drink flowing. The table opposite was laden with sodas for the ladies, whisky, beer and rum for the men who were all gathered in the dining room to the left of the corridor. Raucous laughter and a hybrid of Malayalam and Hebrew burst from the open doorway, punctuated by quavering snatches of old Jewish songs. They sang of love, of marriage.

A slightly giddy Gamy tottered over. His glasses had slipped down his nose and his long front teeth seemed to have lengthened with the influence of drink. Armed with a Coke, he led me into the dining room where I sat next to him, Johnny and Isaac Joshua from Ernakulam. By the look of them all, either I was very late or they had started very early. Around thirty men, Black and White, Indian and foreign guests, sat around the huge table that was used for formal banquets. A Star of David light twinkled on the wall opposite. The men started another round of singing, thumping the table as they sang, each trying to outdo the other, even the gentle Isaac Ashkenazi joined in, never happier than when he was surrounded by rowdy male company and safe from the perilous grasp of predatory females. In the absence of Sammy, Isaac from Ernakulam led the festivities. In a room full of voices, his bellowed the loudest.

The ladies flitted in and out, bearing great platters of hot food, a fabulous spread of tongue-lashing chilly chicken curry, delicately spiced kidneys with onion, tomato and finely chopped dhania, rice, salads, pastels and pickles. In the name of a couple far away, a couple most had never met, they united in celebration. Isaac ordered a replenishment of plates and glasses. Then in the soft haze of satisfaction, it was time for the community to offer prayers for the couple. Unsteadily he rose to his feet, passed his hand over his smooth bald head as if for good luck and began to read from the Torah, voice trembling with the melody of its meaning. His audience was overcome; a couple of the men snuffled into their hankies. It cannot have escaped them that this was a wedding that should have taken place in Cochin or that there never would be another wedding on this street in their lifetime or their children's. Isaac led the prayers for more than thirty minutes. Gamy, ever the provocateur, said he couldn't remember all the words, only to receive a look of severe remonstration from Isaac which was enough to bend him into submission. For this was the nature of family: united in a tumultuous shared history, yet distinct in nature and temperament; rousing camaraderie one minute and irritating the hell out of one another the next; capable of love despite having hurt one another. For the first time since I arrived in Cochin, that night around Johnny and Juliette's table the Black and White Jews were one, grievances forsaken like false lovers and the past a forgotten territory. There could be no better wedding gift for a young couple in Israel.

* * * *

As the men sang late into the night, the women remembered weddings past. They were no different to womenfolk of any community: talk centered on what outfit the bride might wear, the ceremony and love songs. I looked at Juliette, who was happy that the party had been successful, cheeks blushed with pleasure. Her daughter Yaheh also seemed very much at peace as she gently stroked Baby Doll's fur and laughed with the others. Keith had not come that night, nor his brother Len. Pretty much everyone else was there, yet they remained the invisible men of Synagogue Lane.

In the old days marriages were arranged and there was little say in the matter for the youngsters. It was the Indian as well as the Jewish way then. Once the bride's family had received a proposal and accepted, the people of Jew Town would gather and summon the couple to its presence. The foremost elder would ask the groom if the match met his parents' wishes and then he would ask of the young man's own wish, to which he replied simply: "I desire her."

Once the engagement was toasted, the women would bake sesame cookies as a symbol of fertility and a wedding date was fixed. In the community's heyday, it was said that the bridal outfit of the Cochini Jews was known for its exceptional finery. The fabric for her skirt was silk lined with cotton, stretched tight on a wooden frame and hand-embroidered by the Muslim dressmakers who were known for their intricate needle-work. The wedding blouse was sheer white muslin, edged with gold, and upon her head the bride would wear a cap decorated with more gold jewelry or embroidery. On her neck she wore the *kali mala*, a heavy beaded necklace made up of pearls or gold coins or sometimes squares of turtle shell. Before the wedding, the local goldsmith would come to the bridal home and in the presence of the couple and their families he would fashion the ring from a gold coin provided by the groom's father. The traditional Hindu bridal necklace, the *tali mala*, made of gold and inlaid gems, was then clasped around the bride's neck by the groom's sister. This was one Hindu custom that the Kerala Jews adopted.

The road to the synagogue was spread with coconut branches and men were hired to beat drums, while troupes of Hindu musicians played

Jewish wedding songs. The Jews were just one strand of the many religions that had been woven into Kerala's multi-faith history. In Cochin, the Muslim would painstakingly sew the Jewish bride's blouse, while the Hindu would lend his music and song to her wedding procession.

The ceremony took place in the synagogue. Before the groom left his house a lump of sugar was placed in his mouth, so he may always taste the sweetness in life. He would arrive at the synagogue at the head of a procession with a parasol over his head or sometimes hoisted on the shoulders of friends, accompanied by whoops of joy, the rat-tat-tat of firecrackers and lighted torches. The groom was also dressed in white, with a gold-embroidered *kippah* and a garland of flowers around his neck. Years ago, the groom would be attired in a Baghdadi-style silk *kaftan* and white turban. At the synagogue he was received by guests who showered him with bright green leaves and tiny coins.

As he took his place on the *tevah*, the groom looked toward his bride and then recited a love song. Sometimes the congregation would join in. The bride sat on a chair, screened from view by a linen curtain on a circular rail suspended above her head. In the table in front of the Ark was the *ketubah*, the synagogue registry, pen and inkstand. The Cochini ketubah or marriage contract is quite beautiful, lavishly decorated with flowers, birds of paradise and animals as well as auspicious motifs around a central inscription calling upon God to bless the marriage and make it fertile: "Your wife shall be like a fruitful vine within your house; your sons like olive saplings around your table. So shall the man who fears the Lord be blessed."

As happy memories flooded the Hallegua household, I heard the love story of the grandparents of the groom we were toasting. "Now *that* was something," said one of the ladies softly as she smoothed the skirts of her sari. "Baby and Balfour went through so much to be together. See, they were what you people would call a love match."

* * * *

The year was 1950, the era of conservatism, not just in India but in the West. India was still newly independent, yet entrenched in the ancient social traditions and caste boundaries. America's civil rights movement was still nascent; Britain was about to witness seismic changes to its cultural landscape as children of the Empire arrived to make a new life. Yet, just as the Black Jews of Kerala had been early pioneers in their battle for racial equality in the sixteenth century, so they would begin the decade of the 1950s by breaking the last taboo among Black and White Jews.

Balfour was the second son of Ruth and A.B. Salem, the man who did more than anyone to break barriers between the Paradesi and Malabari Jews. Balfour was the one who fought for equality in matters of the heart. A tall man, with slicked black hair and a neat pencil moustache in the style of a silent movie star, he fell in love with Seema "Baby" Koder, who belonged to the White community. She bore the name of one of the great Paradesi clans and she was also a beauty, with expressive dark eyes and a creamy complexion. Baby and Balfour decided they would marry but were coldly informed by the White elders that their marriage could not be held in the Paradesi Synagogue.

Undeterred, they left for Bombay where they married in a Baghdadi Jewish synagogue with only A.B. Salem and his oldest son Raymond in attendance. The bride's family refused to come and the wedding was boycotted by other Cochini Jews who had migrated to Bombay. Their love affair was deemed a scandal which flouted centuries of tradition that decreed that Black and White Jews should never intermarry.

Raymond took the official wedding photograph of the couple. It showed Balfour dressed in a smart white double-breasted suit, with dark cravat and pocket handkerchief and white loafers, looking every inch the sophisticated dandy. A small smile played beneath his moustache as he lent an arm to his bride. Baby wore an ornate lace gown, with a long tulle train. Her hair was pulled back into a loose chignon and held in place with a headpiece of white flowers and lace. Cradled in her arms was a bouquet of white flowers and palm fronds to remind her of home. She was perfect, yet it was not her vestal beauty that struck me while examining the old photo, but the look of defiance written in the soft curves of her face. As if she knew what was coming.

Back in Cochin, the elders reacted with utter disbelief and rage. Keen to scupper the union, a visiting rabbi was consulted on the legality of the marriage, yet he harked back to the sixteenth century rabbinical ruling which said marriage was permissible provided all the proper ceremonies had been carried out.

The couple initially moved to Madras in the neighboring state of Tamil Nadu. Balfour got work as an engineer there and Baby attempted to broker reconciliation with her family through a series of letters. Her family rejected her entreaties. Indeed, the rest of her community decided that if she ever stepped foot in Cochin she should be barred from the Paradesi Synagogue.

As months passed the pain of separation become intolerable. The couple were displaced from their family, their synagogue and yearned to come home. Baby's parents were also missing their daughter and with the approach of Yom Kippur, they relented and invited her to visit.

It should have been a happy homecoming. Yet she was oblivious that the Paradesi elders had passed a motion to bar her from entering the synagogue. As far as they were concerned, she was no longer a White Jew, but a person of no status in their eyes. She was now one of the others. She arrived in time for Yom Kippur but was told by her family and in-laws to avoid the synagogue. The Paradesi elders had already decided that if she arrived to pray, they would stage a walk-out and hold services in Sassoon Hall, a private house a few doors down. In preparation, some of the Torah scrolls had already been taken to the private residence in preparation.

Many would have found such a boycott difficult to bear. But the steely look in Baby's eye hinted she was tougher than anyone imagined. On the day of Shabbat, she walked boldly into the Paradesi Synagogue to take her place upstairs. There was an immediate walkout of both men and women, while one man ordered her to leave. These were people she had grown up with, so the pain and degradation of their rejection must have been deep. Her resolve remained undiminished and she remained in her seat, insisting on her right to pray in the synagogue. They left her to it, unwilling to share the synagogue with what they saw as a tarnished woman. Baby remained where she was and only when she had finished praying did she get up from her seat and leave. It was the Kerala Jews' Rosa Parks moment.

She stood by her principles. Yet for the sake of harmony and perhaps her family, when she visited the Paradesi Synagogue in the future, she did not go upstairs, but sat on a bench downstairs at the back. In old age, she confided to friends and family of the loneliness of those first days of married life and her return to Kerala. After time, the couple relocated to Cochin and many families continued to cut them out of their society. The pettiness of some of her neighbors was vicious, with a few families even refusing to attend any party that Balfour and Baby were invited to. Yet some did accept the marriage and over time life almost returned to normality.

The Salems continued to trail-blaze. Where Balfour went, his younger brother Gamy followed. Gamy and Reema married seven years later in Bombay. But when it came to going to synagogue, Reema simply took a seat downstairs and at the back, explaining that she did not have her sister-in-law's pugnacious spirit.

One account of the story, *Kashrut, Caste and Kaballah* by Katz and Goldberg, tellingly refers to how the young Gamy was so angered by the discrimination of the elders that he boycotted synagogue services for many years. To this day Gamy seemed to have little love for religion, having suffered at first hand the bigotry that was practiced in its name. His sisters went further, marrying outside the Jewish community altogether. Esther married a Hindu and Malkah a Christian.

The prejudice continued to plague the following generation. Baby and Balfour's first son Leslie was banned from being circumcised in the synagogue itself because he was of mixed blood. Instead, the Paradesi elders suggested the ritual take place in Sassoon Hall. The couple was incensed by the suggestion that the ceremony be held in a private house and instead chose to have him circumcised in one of the Malabari synagogues. The stubborn Paradesi elders refused to acknowledge this alternative arrangement and like characters in some black comedy, they remained seated in silence at Sassoon Hall, hosting a circumcision banquet in the absence of the child and his parents.

It took a full generation for equality to arrive in matters of love. When Leslie grew up and in turn married Glennis Simon, another White Jewess, things had moved on considerably from the time of his parents' wedding. Everyone, Black and White, came to celebrate the marriage in 1978. The last taboo had been irrevocably destroyed.

But by then it was too late to make any difference to the community's future. After millennia of Jewish refugees coming to Kerala's shores, the tide of migration had turned back towards Israel. Within a decade or so, most of the community was gone. Balfour, Baby, Leslie and Glennis were among those who moved to Israel. Balfour died there but Baby lived to see her grandson's wedding day in the land of their ancient forefathers. *Their* way, the way of all Jews coming together, turned out to be the future. This was what Israel was meant to be. The time of the old Paradesi prejudices was over. Yet the taste of victory was bitter upon their lips.

* * * *

CHAPTER TEN

"A Wife Who Will Not Give Me Headache"

"My rabbi said, 'Settle, settle. What about a woman like Mrs. Blitzstein? She may not be a great beauty, but nobody is better at smuggling food and light firearms in and out of the ghetto' . . . Pity my dilemma, dear reader. Never to find all the requirements one needs in a single member of the opposite sex."

—WOODY ALLEN

After the exodus from Kerala, those left behind faced stark choices, particularly the few youngsters that remained. There were no people in their teens or twenties in the Paradesi community, but among the Malabaris there were some: Babu's girls, another three daughters in the old Jewish village of Parul and the Abraham boys, Anil and Solomon.

Solomon had already left Cochin for Chennai where he worked. I met Anil at the wedding celebration at Johnny's house. He and his brother spent most of the night watching cricket, whooping with delight, but later that evening as we chatted he offered to take me around Cochin the next day to show me the old villages of Parul and Chennamangalam.

Anil was the eldest son of Samuel Abraham, who had moved to Israel before coming home again, disenchanted with what he discovered there. Anil's maternal grandfather was the leading elder of the Malabar Jews, Isaac Joshua, who was fiercely protective of his community's legacy. Anil grew up in the heart of this influential family, built on devotion to one another and to the faith. At the Shimni/Simhat Torah celebration a few evenings before, I met Anil for the first time. While the Paradesi Synagogue had been dressed for the occasion and dazzled, the Ernakulam place of worship was simply lit and furnished with a few garlands of fresh jasmine. In some ways it reflected the respective personalities of the communities themselves. That night I watched a young man who had inherited his grandfather's combination of great seriousness and purpose with an ability to find humor in everything. He was a natural optimist and seemed to infect everyone with his easy manner. He had the potential to take over from Isaac Joshua, I thought, if there was anything left to lead by that time. After the prayer ceremony, Anil had assisted his grandfather and father in preparing for the blessings at the dinner table before we sat down to a Simhat Torah feast for the Malabaris and their friends, with forty of us—Jews and non-Jews—around the table. Here, Anil was at his most contented—in the synagogue anteroom, eating fire-breathing curry, singing old Hebrew songs as his raucous grandfather thumped the table to keep time. After a few drinks, as everyone melted into conviviality, he would cast a shy glance towards the girls at the other end of the table, slowly passing a hand over his hair, smoothing it down.

Over the years the family had constructed a very happy and comfortable life in a suburb near Ernakulam. They had a successful business now and Anil was working as a tour guide. It earned him top dollar rates and the only thing left was to find a wife and settle down.

In any other society his options would be good. He was in his late twenties, from a respectable family and with a well paid job. His two biggest attributes were his likeability and his integrity. He lived part of his childhood in Israel until the family came back. But unlike many others, Anil had no desire to leave India again. His heart was bound to Kerala. As we walked along the riverbank not far from the historic Jewish village of Parul, he told me of his dilemma. He loved it here. The food, the people, the land. The smell of pepper that grew in long curling strands on the trees all around us. Walking through ankle-deep grass along the river banks, sheltered by the shade of tall slender palms and pepper trees. Watching the narrow-boats dotting the river, as fishermen draw nets like water-spangled cobwebs from the water. When Anil felt pressured, "when I need to breathe" as he put it, he would climb into his car and drive for thirty minutes to a spot like this, where little had changed in a hundred years. He stretched out his hand and snatched a strand of green peppercorns from a nearby tree, like a tiny beaded necklace in his palm.

Anil was truly a man of Cochin. In a world where everyone seemed to want more, he told me he had enough. Nothing could match what he had been born to. And yet, for all this, he was seriously considering going to Israel to find a bride. It was all that was missing. I asked him about the prospects for marriage here and he shook his head, rubbing the peppercorn necklace between finger and thumb, the friction releasing its pungent smell from the small green beads. His family had exhausted all options, not just in Kerala where they were few, but even as far as Bombay, which was home to the Bene Israel Jews.

"I don't wish to go, you understand. But I must look at my choices. Here there's no chance to find a wife."

When I asked him what he looked for in a bride, he didn't say she must be pretty, or rich or educated. His requirements were fairly uncomplicated.

"A Jewish wife who will not give me headache," he said, and then laughed, as if embarrassed, as if he'd wished for the ridiculous.

* * * *

He slipped the necklace into his pocket and we got back into the car to drive to the old Parul synagogue. Once it had been the most beautiful of all the eight places of worship in Kerala. The beautiful carved wooden Ark, engraved with flowers and leaves and topped with a crown, had been dismantled and taken to the Israel Museum years ago. Like the Paradesi synagogue, from its ceiling was suspended a myriad of glass lanterns of different colors, yet Parul's structure was unsound and the Jews could not muster funds to save it. Anil hoped that by showing all this to visiting Israelis and Jews from around the world, he could raise awareness and perhaps someone would offer to fund their restoration.

According to Jussay's *The Jews of Kerala*, Parul was the second oldest synagogue after the ones in Cranganore, supposedly containing two Torah scrolls brought from Shingly after the destruction by the Moors in the sixteenth century. Jussay relates a story about how the synagogue fell into disuse after the Jews of Parul, angered by the Christians, offered incense in mockery of Christian worship. For this act of sacrilege, they were punished with the plague, he said. Their synagogue fell into disuse and the *ner tamid* or Eternal Lamp was hung in the street as a sign of contrition. It was rebuilt in 1616 by Jacob Castiel, leader of the Jewish community in Cochin.

The Parul Jews had further run-ins with some Christians who tried to disrupt their worship by loudly banging drums outside the synagogue during Shabbat. Frustrated, the Jews turned to the Viceroy of India who was visiting Travancore at the time. The Jews gained an audience with the Viceroy who was sympathetic and he ordered the erection of two stone pillars at the road entering Jew Street to bar traffic. The Jews hailed this as a victory.

We pulled up outside Jew Street, just in front of its famous pillars. A white goat was tied to the synagogue's entrance gates, which were locked. Anil went to talk to the neighbor who warned him that the place had become infested with cobras and that there were so many they were infiltrating his house through the broken boundary walls.

We went to the gate and unlocked it, passing the goat on our way. Lying between us and the synagogue itself was a vast overgrown garden. The grass was almost waist-high in places, brown and tangled bushes engulfed the pathway which was no longer visible. If one looked carefully at the ground, one could discern pale gold translucent husks of old snake skins. The synagogue lay some fifty yards ahead. Nobody came here anymore, so no one knew what state it was in. In a few years, with the entire community gone, would this be the fate of all the synagogues?

The goat bleated in fear, warning us not to go any further. Anil told me the neighbors also had warned against it. "They killed two cobras in the last week alone. Both came through the crack in the synagogue wall," he said. Now the goat was pulling wildly at its tethers, slipping and sliding as it attempted to move away from the gate. I wanted to see inside, but not enough to make that walk. "If you're ready to meet your relatives and your maker, we can go see it," joked Anil. "Although, I'm not quite ready yet."

We heeded the goat's counsel in the end and padlocked the gate again. Mightily relieved, the goat settled back into his spot and watched us leave. All the houses in Parul's Jew Town were now in the hands of Hindus and Christians. No Jews were left and the synagogue was the only reminder of what once was.

Now, he was taking me to meet his grandmother's brother who lived not far from the other Jewish village of Chennamangalam. This particular village had done much better in the lottery of preservation. It won a grant from the Indian government to restore the synagogue. Next to the synagogue was the oldest Jewish tombstone in Kerala, dated 1269. It was inscribed in Hebrew with "Sara bat Israel" or Sara, daughter of Israel. This was one of the oldest proofs of the antiquity of the Jewish community in Cochin. The synagogue's foundations were said to date back to sixteenth century. But Chennamangalam had another claim to fame. It was also a symbol of religious tolerance. One story of the village said a former maharajah wished to have each of the four major faiths represented in this place and so designated four points for the construction of a synagogue, a Christian church, a Hindu temple and a mosque. It was said that at the axis that formed the center of these cardinal points, he built a palace.

The four places of worship lie within one kilometer of one another and the locals claim it is the only village in the world where one can hear the *shofar* of the synagogue, the peel of the church bell, the trumpet of the Hindu conch shell and the cry of the *muezzin*.

Not far from here was the house of Anil's grandmother's brother, the eighty-two-year-old Menachem who was born in Chennamangalam itself. It was set in a wild garden full of pepper, tamarind and fruit trees. Jackfruits and papaya lay strewn on the ground ready to be collected, a kitchen garden of herbs grew in fragrant profusion in a corner. Black chickens scuttled back and forth from shade to bush and back again as they made brief forays for tidbits.

The house was newly renovated, with a porch and tiled floor throughout. In the front parlor was an elaborately carved three piece sofa set and a coffee table already laden with ladoos, deep fried banana chips and other snacks, plus chai. The old man sat in an armchair. He had a fine head of grey hair and a broad physique, strong and muscled apart from his right leg which was withered after a childhood bout of polio. He tucked the leg back, hiding it from view beneath the folds of his *lunghi*. Menachem spoke in a high speed, voluble manner, periodically stopping to laugh at his jokes as he wiped his eyes. He was charming and a born story teller, accompanying his tale with fearsome gesticulation.

I was here to listen to the story of a historic feud between Parul and Chennamangalam which stemmed from one of the most bizarre episodes in Kerala Jewish history. It was known as "Sarah's story" and Sarah was a distant relative of Menachim, so who better to tell it. As I listened to the tale, I decided that Sarah would not have been Anil's kind of woman, being the kind of Jewish wife who induced not just "headaches", but crippling migraines.

Sarah was a beautiful Jewess from a very wealthy landowning family in Parul. At a very young age she married an equally rich man from a family in Chennamangalam but was widowed a few years later after giving birth to two daughters. It was a difficult position for a young widow to be in. She was still young and very desirable, with the added complication that she was extremely rich. Her daughters would inherit a joint estate, which also made them targets for suitors.

Her late husband's family was keen to marry the daughters to their own young men, thereby securing the fortune. But Sarah's brothers demanded the same, so with the seeming wisdom of Solomon, Sarah offered to give one daughter to Parul and the other to Chennamangalam. However, neither side was satisfied, so she incurred the wrath of both.

In a further attempt to wrest control of her wealth, the relatives argued that Sarah was unfit to manage her money and offered to take control of her business affairs. But she was having none of it and decided to employ a poor Jew from Chennamangalam to assist her. She began to mix with people from all levels of society, further enraging the family who claimed she was damaging her reputation.

Jussay wrote about the episode which seemed to include all the ingredients for a primetime soap opera. The otherwise dry historian reported breathlessly: "They deliberately spread scandals about her. She was depicted as a shameless slut tarnishing the image of the entire Jewish community. Her own behavior gave credence to these stories." The historian seemed to have some sympathy with her relatives, adding reprovingly, "She used to stay away from home for days together and used to welcome home visitors during odd hours."

One of those visitors who stayed "suspiciously long" was Thomman, a Christian leader from Gothuruth, a village of daring zealots who modeled themselves on the exploits of the Red Cross Knights of Europe. Thomman and his friends formed their own Round Table of Knights, says Jussey, vowing to defend their faith with the sword and protect damsels in distress and the like. This fabulous medieval-style religious intrigue took place in the midst of Kerala's tropical countryside just one hundred years ago.

So here was our heroine, the Jewess widow, young, rich, gorgeous and refusing to deny herself any of life's pleasures to the incandescence of her male relatives. Thomman was everything they despised: a tall, athletic Christian with his own private posse. I asked Menachem about the relationship between Sarah and Thomman and the old man looked coy and blushed a little, so we shall have to turn to Jussay's version of events. "The two became intimate," he said delicately and their behavior sent the elders into a fury. The result was a boycott of Sarah.

But things got even more complicated. Sarah found out she was pregnant, although it is unclear by whom. She avoided scandal by marrying her footman. When the Jews of the two villages found out their seething resentment boiled over into rage. They seized her unlucky husband and thrashed him by the riverside. A friend of Thomman found him and took care of him and then Thomman offered Sarah his protection and invited her to stay at his home where she would be safe.

Her life was now in danger and there were rumors that the Jewish elders would snatch her girls to save them from associated scandal. Sarah, her husband and the girls went to live with Thomman, her lover. The set-up was too much for the Jewish elders, who gathered a group at Cochin, collected firearms and weapons and set out by rowboat to Gothuruth to abduct the daughters and mother. Their plan was foiled when they were spotted by Thomman's brother, who raised the alarm.

Sarah ran to the rice pounding shed and hid, the girls went upstairs and bolted the room shut. The local Christians came to her aid, gathering makeshift weapons of poles, crowbars, choppers and spades. Menachem described how the attempted snatch failed:

> "One of the brothers came inside. He was holding Sarah and trying to bring her and the children forcibly. One Christian came in and told the brother to let go of her. The brother refused and said 'I'm taking her now.' So this person chopped the brother's arm with a knife. After this, the Jews decided there should be no survivors and the Jews and their helpers sealed all the exits to the village. One of my uncles was killed in this battle—my father's brother."

Overpowered and outfoxed, the Jews fled to the boat but it was pulled ashore and smashed to pieces by the Christians. By now many men of the local village had returned from the bazaar and joined the fray, assailing the Jews in the water with blows from oars and poles. Disgraced and battered, the Jews were forced to retreat. The Jews turned to the courts for help but were rebuffed because the court ruled the Christians acted in self-defense.

"A lot of people died," said Menachem sadly. "The people who came to take her lost their fight. The Jews were jailed for two or three years. My father was also punished; he was just eighteen years old. It was a shameful case, forcefully done," said the old man, wrinkling his nose in distaste. "A shameful way to treat a woman."

In the end, through sheer force of character, she won and her story was immortalized in a ballad called "The Victory of Sarah." She lived to an old age and her wishes regarding her daughters were fulfilled. One married into Parul, one into Chennamangalam. But the scandal took years to die down. Despite being cut off by her community, she brought up her daughters and educated them well and one of her granddaughters became one of the first Malabari Jews to get a university degree.

Yet the people of both villages saw Sarah's story as more than a little shameful. They believed her liberal attitude set a bad example to the younger relatives. I asked what that meant, only for the Anil to gently admonish me: "You have had the whole cake. It is just the cherry on top that's been removed."

As we left his uncle's house at sundown, it was clear Anil had some sympathies with Sarah's male relatives. She had been a handful and they were only doing their duty to protect her and the children.

"Even some modern girls can be like this," he told me gravely. "A *big* headache. It's not something I want. I don't want any trouble when I get married."

"So will you go to Israel to find a wife?"

"A Kerala Jewish girl would be the best for me. But there are no Kerala Jewish girls. I have to find a wife from outside Kerala who wants to come here. But it's not easy. A person used to Indian culture finds western culture difficult to accept. Some people see us as primitive, it's not that. This life is just a village life, no tension."

"Do you think a bride from Israel would find it difficult to adjust?"

"For me it's the ultimate. When I look around, nowhere is more beautiful than this. Just look," he gestured to all around us. "But if I was brought up in Israel, it would've been a different situation. I'm very happy living here. I never had any racial discrimination, I have a lot of

Muslim, Hindu, Christian friends. They tell me, 'why go to Israel?' But I need a wife."

"She couldn't come here?"

"Everything changes. The whole lifestyle changes. I was born and brought up in Israel as a boy—I know the lifestyle and tastes there. Then I came to India, so for me, it's not difficult to adjust. For them, it's difficult. If you're jumping down the ladder, it's different. I cannot ask an Israeli girl, I cannot ask her to give up her Western life for the village. I would have to be very lucky to find a girl such as this."

"But many Israelis love India."

"Loving India and living in India is different."

We were now driving through a stretch of waterways that led directly towards the sea. Black clouds tumbled like boulders across the horizon, swiftly blotting out the last vestiges of light. The biggest storm for months was descending. We could hear the low roll of thunder from just across the hillside and in just a few minutes the whole sky would turn white with sheet and forked lightening. Anil already knew he had to leave. The choice was not really between Kerala and marriage. He could always marry a non-Jewish girl here and stay. The choice was more fundamental, being between Kerala and his Jewishness. He had to lose one part of himself.

"This place, always, it absorbs you. But this is it. Either I choose a bride who is not Jewish, or leave Kerala forever. That's the saddest part of all," said Anil. "You can't gain without compromise. If you want to live in Kerala, you have to compromise on the Jewishness. If you're not willing to compromise on the Jewishness, you cannot live in Kerala. That's the choice we face."

"They should be queuing to come," I told him as we bumped along the road home. Even in this unremitting onslaught of rain, the panorama that enveloped us was dramatic, primal, eternal. The storm had knocked out the electricity, plunging every house, every business, every road into utter darkness, turning sky, mountain and sea into a single entity of black. For a split second, the crackle of lightning illuminated the palm-fringed horizon that stretched before us, seemingly without end. Then it was gone again. Anil knew what he was about to lose.

"They should be queuing, it's true," he replied, struggling to see the road ahead as it became engulfed with fast flowing channels of rainwater that ran down the road in quicksilver streams. "But in order to win, we have to find the exceptions in life. The Jewish girl who will sacrifice everything for Kerala. But we can't always find the exceptions. If I want to live this Jewish life I must leave everything I love. For Israel."

* * * *

CHAPTER ELEVEN

Roses in the Desert

"The sparrow has found his home at last,
The swallow, a nest for its young."
—PSALM 84:3

D awn had not come. Yet it was close at hand and the nightly solitude of the Negev would be broken soon as the sun emerged from behind the mountains. For now, the trunk road that snaked through the desert was desolate, but in less than an hour there would be juddering convoys heading for the ports, army trucks moving towards military checkpoints in the south and carloads of commuters shuttling between Jerusalem and Tel Aviv. As the clouds of night dissipated like djinns shrinking away to their daytime lairs, the skies softened to a near translucent grey and an immeasurable serenity emanated from the barren plains. When the sun finally surfaced, blinking into the new day, the grey skyline was streaked with stripes of candy pink. Set ablaze by the light, the desert came alive.

The plains reached across an expanse of terrain from the Dead Sea down towards the blue finger of the Indian Ocean that pointed to Israel's southernmost tip, Eilat. Flanked to the east by mountains beyond which lay Jordan and to the west by Egypt and the Palestinian territory of Gaza, this was pioneer country. When the first *moshavs* came here in the early fifties, they were equipped with little more than a determination to succeed and from the sands they had summoned up whole communities.

By their very existence here they believed they were defending their country's borders, bringing a Jewish presence after centuries of exile. Some of the *moshavs* were within striking distance of the rocket launchers from Gaza, the ceaseless fear of attack, of being supplanted from these soils, was coupled with the challenge of inducing the unyielding desert to bear life and hope. In spite of these challenges, perhaps even because of them, many, including the Cochini Jews, welcomed the chance to settle here, even above the holy city of Jerusalem, for the desert held an older and equally sacred significance for them.

Abraham, the patriarch of the Jewish people known as "father of the multitude", was inextricably linked with the Negev and specifically to the ancient city of Be'er Sheva, the capital of the region. The meaning of Be'er Sheva was "well of the swearing" which referred to a past agreement between Abraham and a local ruler Abimelech under which the prophet gained rights to use a well to water his flock.

By emulating the life of the prophet, returning here was imbued with additional religious significance. The sacrifice went beyond the merely physical and was a living metaphor for the Jewish struggle. In the past the desert was seen as a place of death and chaos, a desolate void. Biblical descriptions depicted a place of "howling wilderness", "a land unsown", which appeared to have been abandoned by all things good. It was a visceral reminder of the despair endured by the ancient Jews during their forty-year sojourn in the desert before they were led to the Promised Land and the fulfillment and realized destiny that ensued.

There was a brief moment after 1948 when the Cochini Jews feared they would not be allowed to make the *aliyah* after all. Before being granted permission to resettle, the Cochinis were visited by an official from the Jewish Agency on behalf of the nascent state. In his report, he voiced grave concerns about the suitability of this people to settle in Israel. In particular, he was worried about their small stature, weak constitution and the high prevalence of elephantiasis among their number, fearing this would spread to the motherland. The "Report on the Jews of Malabar" described them as small in stature, weak and thin with many suffering from "a disease transmitted via mosquito larvae deposited on the skin at night and which burrow in through the moisture from the sleeper's perspiration." It added: "... More than 50 percent of all Jewish families ... subsist ... under acute want ... the majority live on rice and fish ... malnutrition is widespread." An Israeli physician recommended that the Cochinis were resettled in very dry regions, with great variations in temperature which would minimize the risk of the condition spreading. For this reason, many ended up in the Negev.

In a later report in 1949, the official said he feared the Cochinis were unrealistic about the tough conditions they would face. The officials lectured the Cochinis that they would have to work very hard as farmers in Israel. But the idealistic joy of the Jews of Kerala could not be dampened. All they could focus on was finally going home.

On arrival, it proved to be every bit as tough as the Israeli officials had forewarned. In particular, the Cochinis found it difficult to adjust to living in a country that constantly had to be braced for battle. In the

1973 account *Immigrants from India in Israel* by Gilbert Kushner, the author described a night patrol with a Cochini guard on his round at 2:00 AM:

> "Aaron, one of the Cochini on guard duty tonight, is especially concerned about not tripping in the darkness for he is carrying a loaded rifle and wearing a heavy cartridge belt. He holds the weapon clumsily as if it were a piece of wood. I ask him to make sure the safety lever is on ... On the way back up the hill, Aaron tells me this never happened in Cochin ..."

The vast majority of Cochini Jews settled in *moshavs* across the southern region, with several settlements that were almost exclusively theirs. These were complete townships with their own residential district, shops and even synagogue all a short drive away from Be'er Sheva. Sixty years on, these communities were rejuvenated and replenished by new marriages and births. In one *moshav* in the south of the Negev, the Cochinis had created a facsimile of their old land which they called Little Kerala. The fear of demise that afflicted the people in India no longer tormented those resettled in Israel. The *aliyah* had facilitated a rebirth for the Jews of Kerala.

The transition from India to Israel was all the more remarkable when one considered that they had not come from, say, the Rajasthan desert, but had traded a land blessed with fertility for the austerity of the Negev. Many of the Cochinis had rarely ventured beyond southern India, so they could never have envisioned what they were letting themselves in for. They never knew the true meaning of desert, only the Biblical depictions of suffering followed by deliverance. The sense of excitement on arriving in the land of Abraham was accompanied by an initial sense of dislocation. It was a natural response; being the opposite of everything they had every known: water, trees, flowers, where life is taken for granted. Into the cracked and hardened landscape, they had to discover ways of instilling some of the vibrancy, fertility and life of their old home.

There, they had had every natural advantage. Throw a seed to the ground, leave it untouched, unnourished by human hand and it will flourish and proliferate. In Kerala they luxuriated in an abundance of water and its gifts whether it was the Arabian Sea, the lotus-strewn lakes or backwaters shaded by tendrils of tropical flowers that cascaded into the water. If they desired milk, there were buffalos who ambled like stately *mehmsahibs* in the surrounding fields. If they wanted fruits and vegetables, then they only need step into their gardens. In Israel, the Jews of Cochin were tested. It proved to be the making of some of them.

I was driving to Shahar to meet one such man. Eliahu Bezalel had come to Israel in the very first wave of Cochini immigration in the early 1950s. In India he had been, by his own admission, a young man of little consequence but larger ambition, with just a few rupees in his pocket when he embarked on the *aliyah*. On arrival, like many of the first pioneers, his first job seemed to hold little promise of achievement or greatness. He was a shepherd and he carried out his duty with diligence and pride, for even the smallest task was part of the wider effort to build Israel. This was the homecoming they had prayed for in Kerala for two thousand years: "Next year, in Jerusalem," they toasted one another at each festival.

Shahar was more than an hour and a half from Jerusalem on the road to Be'er Sheva, off the turning towards Gaza. After interminable

175

vistas of reds and browns, breathing in air acrid as the ochre dust that enveloped the horizon, the landscape melted into a shimmer of softest green. As my Palestinian taxi driver Nazeeh drove into the heart of the community, all around we could see long white, tent-like nurseries that sheltered fragile seedlings. The trees, shrubs and lawns were verdant, not the washed out brown-green that forever thirsts for rain, but with the vividness of a freshly watered springtime. The settlement was made up of suburban avenues, some complete with idyllic white picket fences and lawns nourished by sprinkler systems that could put the proudest English country gardener to shame. Whitewashed bungalows with not a tile out of place were set in neat rows with well groomed gardens. Framing the roadside were bushes of billowing roses and fig trees, fragrant with ripened fruit. With eyes hypnotized by the suburban utopia, one could almost forget this was a desert of the East until one's gaze was drawn to the middle horizon beyond the white fences. There lay the realities that the inhabitants kept at bay every day, relentless desert dunes and the blur of low mountain ridges that signaled the Jordanian border. Away from the *moshav* dream, underlying every Jew's romantic ambition to make the desert of the Holy Land bloom, there was the unceasing nature of the struggle to conserve life in these lands and the vulnerability of its tightly drawn borders.

Nazeeh was surprised as he slowly drove past the pretty houses, with children playing outside, their chocolate drop eyes, glossy dark skin and black kinked hair all signs that we were in the right place. With its palms, bougainvillea and tropical flowers, this could still be India. The Cochinis had created a corner of Kerala in the Israeli desert, even copying the village style bungalow with sloping red tiled roofs and wide pillared porches to snatch at a passing breeze. Just as in Kerala, rambling bushes trailed trains of pink blossom over low-rise walls. Flocks of sparrows chirruped among the date palms, periodically taking off to skim the skies in tight triangular formations like Israeli Air Defense squadrons on patrol.

Amidst the loveliness was the house of Bezalel, the prettiest and with the most well kept of all the gardens, as if it belonged in a postcard. A young man who looked like a Cochin Jew squatted low among the flower beds, his forearms a burnished copper as he wrenched out stubborn weeds, shook their tangled roots free and tilled the soil. The sheen of sweat was evident on his skin as the white disc of the sun burned overhead. His face was shielded from the rays in a large brimmed straw hat, affording only a view of pursed lips and set jaw as he concentrated on the task at hand. Seeing strangers, he paused from digging, looked up and smiled, his teeth bright and dazzling, before turning back to the flowerbeds. I was to learn that this was Bezalel's young son, who lived in the next door house and was taking over the running of the family's horticultural business.

The old man himself was inside in the shade of the kitchen that overlooked the rear garden. He was recovering from a recent operation on his knee a few weeks ago. It had left him housebound and only able to walk with the aid of a walking frame. Bezalel was in his late seventies but retained a touch of the rakish handsomeness that was evident in the gallery of photographs that lined the walls of his house, ones where as a young man in black suit and skinny tie he posed jauntily with Israeli leaders shortly after his arrival. Further along the wall, there were modern day portraits of him receiving awards and medals from the president of India or prime minister of Israel for services to horticulture or Indo-Israeli relations.

From being a poor young émigré from India with just 250 rupees in his pocket on arrival in the country, he had become an ambassador for the Indian Jewish community, a flesh and blood emblem of the success that can come from simple hard work and devotion. Stepping into his home, one could smell the pungent tang of curry powder in the air: cumin, coriander, black pepper—the smells of Cochin's tropical marketplace wafting on Middle Eastern desert winds. These same smells first enticed the merchant seamen of King Solomon to India's shores almost three millennia ago.

His wife and daughter, old and younger versions of the same woman, were rustling around the kitchen, laying out the requisite snacks and drinks of iced lemonade with chopped fresh mint before heading off to their lunchtime appointments. Bezalel sat with me at the table, now spread with homemade cakes, pastries and deliciously tart sliced apple from the Golan Heights. His face was worn with pain and as he rested his hands on the kitchen table, I noticed his fingernails were blackened from recent treatment for prostate cancer, although it was something he barely touched on.

For despite illness, the physical discomfort and pain he bore, one sensed Bezalel was a man fulfilled, whose young man's ambition had been sated. First he had made the journey from India to Israel. Then he had risen from ordinary shepherd, to soldier, to businessman to ambassador not just for his new country, but for Kerala. From this tiny agricultural community in the Negev, as small and unremarkable as any Indian village, Bezalel had accomplished much and reached beyond his narrow world into one where he consorted with leaders and delivered lectures on his business and Indo-Jewish culture to audiences from Jerusalem to Delhi to Washington.

The source of all this was a simple idea from an ordinary man. Bezalel had won his fame by making the wastelands of the Negev bloom. He had brought roses to the desert. And even better than that, he helped turn it into one of the biggest exports of the Israeli economy. Now in his late seventies, he could contemplate a legacy that went beyond mere commerce. He was married to a Cochini Jewess called Batzion and they had four children: two sons and two daughters. Last, but most important of all, he was a grandfather. He took none of this for granted, especially when he heard of how things had worked out in his old country. But when he left in the fifties, such things were not on the mind of a young man looking for adventure.

Every Jew who came to Israel harbored different motives in their hearts. Bezalel left his village of Chennamangalam, the village that was home to four great religions, with the aim of living the Zionist dream. He fervently believed in Zionism, indeed, the Cochini Jews had grown up with it branded on their consciousness even before the horrors of the Second World War. They lived in a place where the Jews had never been persecuted. They never encountered the cold fear that so many of their brethren lived with elsewhere in the world. They had lived alongside Hindu, Muslim and Christian for millennia in India, free to be Jewish as well as Indian. And yet the Zionist dream lived on in the hearts of men like Bezalel. It harked back to the days when the Second Temple was broken and the Jews were driven out. They never forgot that Cochin, or "Little Jerusalem" as they sometimes called it, was only a facsimile of that past life.

Cecil Koder, one of the old Cochini residents, wrote a poem in the 1930s that summed up their feelings:

> *"It is our sincere ambition,*
> *To be freed from foreign domination.*
> *Palestine is our inspiration,*
> *To build our home, a Jewish nation.*
> *For God is always on our side,*
> *He is our sincere guide,*
> *Then why should we fear,*
> *When we have Him near,*
> *In days of sorrow and darkness.*
> *We have passed through darker situation,*
> *And won for us thrilling admiration,*
> *Jerusalem is our destination.*
> *The home and hope of our salvation.*
> *Now we make an open declaration*
> *To every anti-Jewish nation,*
> *All their baseless, ruthless persecution*
> *Will never bring our ruination."*

The words seemed grimly prophetic of what was to come in Europe. What struck me reading the poem was the sense of unwavering determination. The source went way back, to the beginning. For men like Koder and Bezalel, Zionism was not born of their experiences in India; the Jews had been well loved by the Indians. It was a matter of righting the wrongs of a broader history. "It was pure Zionism," Bezalel said as he explained his motivation to come here, "to build the country."

At the start of the 1940s there were around two thousand Jews in Cochin. After the formation of the state of Israel in 1948, the migration began in earnest in 1950 and within a few decades there were fewer than fifty Jews left in Kerala. The primary reason to go was to return to the land of their forefathers. But they were also driven to leave by poor economic prospects. Their economic decline began once the British Empire made the port cities of Bombay and Calcutta central to their trading business, reducing Cochin's importance. In 1947 India won its independence from Britain and as a new secular democracy the old system of colonial rule and princely states bestowing privileges on favorites became a thing of the past. Kerala was now part of the new India and the special privileges that had been enjoyed by the Jews from the time of Joseph Rabban were abolished.

The Cochini Jews lost out on trade, then the nascent Indian government further impeded their business with a ban on the import of luxury goods. The state Communist government also nationalized key industries and businesses, such as the ferry service in Kerala which had been a profitable Jewish-owned concern. In 1957 private land estates were seized, nationalized and redistributed among the population, including that of the old Jewish land barons. This was followed in 1979 by the nationalization of the Jewish-run electric company.

The old certainties were gone forever. The young looked around them in India and saw that the economic and political privileges that had taken centuries to build were now stripped away. Not that the Jews were specifically targeted in any way. It was all part of a wider political dynamic underway.

Then there was the issue of marriage. Even by the fifties, intermarriage between Black and White was taboo. This reduced the choice of marriage partners for the young and the pressure to conform to the way of the elders continued to be suffocating. Whenever the Black and White Jews came together, their past joined them like a difficult and unwanted guest at the dinner table.

The prospect of a new country, a Jewish homeland which needed people to build an infrastructure, industry, communities from scratch was appealing to many of the Cochini Jews, particularly those with little money, land or prospects in India. Israel also represented a new beginning in another key way. It was a country for all Jews, regardless of color or ethnicity. The Black Jews in particular, saw a chance for a future unencumbered by the prejudices of the past. For all the above reasons— Zionism, faith, economics, marriage and freedom—many Jews decided to quit Kerala forever.

Some of the older guard feared the "new exodus", as they termed it, was evidence of the old curse on the Kerala Jews reasserting itself. Those left behind lamented that their past sins were being paid for as they watched loved ones pack up and go. The answer to this fatalism may be to look at what happened to the Cochini Jews once they settled in Israel.

It proved to be a renaissance of sorts. Today, there are 5,000 Jews in Israel with Cochini blood. Their numbers are spread all over the country, from the northernmost border with Lebanon to *moshavs* deep in the Negev as well as pockets of communities in Haifa and Jerusalem. As Bezalel told me, this blossoming of the Kerala Jews in Israel sprang from the dust beneath their feet when families like his arrived in the 1950s.

* * * *

"It was totally barren, there was *nothing*," said Bezalel, gently grazing his grey stubble with black fingernails. "We lived in a small wooden structure of twenty-six square meters for each family. That was the only thing. In three years we built the first proper house with the help of the Jewish Agency. And in 1958 I married Batzion in this village. She's from the Mattancherry community," he told me.

Such were the foundations of a new life. In the first years of marriage, the couple purchased land and experimented with a new agricultural business. At the time there were sixty families in the *moshav*, most of whom were North African Jews. Gradually, more Cochini families came to settle here and the two communities bonded.

"They didn't know where we came from. They didn't know of India's ancient culture or its history of Jews, so at first they kept their distance. After some years we settled and it came to the point where we, the Co-chinis, were the first to lead the whole village towards development."

Bezalel proved to be a natural leader and businessman. He started by growing flowers for export. It was a new venture and would have been risky even in the most benevolent of climates. In the midst of the desert, in a country fighting for its very survival, it seemed a hopeless enterprise. He began with gladioli. By the sixties, Bezalel had achieved the prover-bial-like miracle of selling flowers to Holland and won first prize for ex-porting gladioli from the Israeli prime minister. The central government spotted the wider potential and in 1966 approached him to develop a modern greenhouse industry in the Negev.

"Naturally, I agreed. I went to study greenhouse techniques in Lon-don and Holland. When I came back we started the first modern climate controlled greenhouse in this village. The first in the country," he told me. His eyes sparkled as he recollected the experiment. By growing his gladioli and then selling them overseas, he was playing his part in the Zionist dream of establishing a viable country, with its own industries, pioneering technologies and innovation. Soon, his ambitions moved a gear up. He was ready to move from gladioli to roses.

"It took five years. Then I decided this was a nice area for growing of roses for export. At first I met with skepticism. It was several years before people understood this was a profitable business and then they started to copy."

The export horticultural business developed from these modest beginnings. Neighboring *moshavs* observed the Shahar experiment and followed suit. By then, Bezalel was exporting roses and gladioli to Holland and met increasing demand by building vast greenhouses that ringed the settlement. By this stage the government and export ministry were lending their help and finance to develop the infrastructure to get the industry off the ground. "Within ten to fifteen years Israel became the third largest exporter of flowers to Holland. I was part of that effort," Bezalel explained.

Indeed, flowers became one of the biggest agricultural exports for Israel within the coming decades. The trade that began in Bezalel's back yard had escalated to a scale he never imagined. But decades later his work was partly undone by a combination of technological advance, hyper-inflation and war with Lebanon, which broke out in 1984.

The war's effect was crippling. Conflict with neighbors was an alien concept for the Kerala Jews who had enjoyed peaceful relations for millennia in India with all faiths, including Muslims, apart from very brief periods in history when they came under attack from the Moors and Portuguese.

Inflation rocketed out of control in Israel and the economy was hit hard. People defaulted on loans and as war raged on its northern border, the government struggled to stabilize an economy that was in freefall.

"Many businesses collapsed, many went bankrupt, many committed suicide," Bezalel recalled flatly. Things then improved after a few years as stability returned and exports picked up a little. But by the 1990s, his business faced a new enemy: globalization. Israel's flower growers were priced out of the market by new, cheaper producers from third world countries such as Kenya and Zimbabwe where the cost of production was a faction of Israel's.

"We pay twenty-six dollars a day for a worker and in Africa it is a dollar a day. We have very big payments for water, electricity, for heating or cooling the greenhouses. In Africa they don't have these costs. So they reduced the price. The market price has therefore gone down so much we can't compete. Now everywhere in the Negev you are seeing empty greenhouses; this is the reason. Nobody can compete with that." I had seen the redundant greenhouse tents myself, their billowing, white canopies flapping in the red dust winds.

I asked him what he was doing now. Bezalel still grew his roses on one and a quarter acres but said this summer that too would end. His new business was grapes as well as ginger and tapioca—staples of his native Kerala. "The Brazilians are dying for that. Maybe next year we'll try new crops."

Bezalel was a survivor and therefore suited to this life. He and his family had all adjusted well to the Israeli way. Of his children one had married a Jewish Canadian, one a Bulgarian, and another daughter married a South African. They lived nearby and she ran a Cochini catering business in one of the disused greenhouses catering to Israelis and tourists who wanted to taste Kerala cuisine. Her business was successful and a link to their old heritage.

His family had never had a problem integrating like other Kerala Jews who came here. Bezalel never felt uncomfortable in Israel like some of his old countrymen such as Babu who had been driven to tears when thinking of his experience here.

"What was it like when you first came to Israel?" I asked him. "You came from a country where the Jews had lived for almost two thousand years with no persecution and total security. Here the situation is so different." The Kerala Jews had gone from a life of peace to one of almost perpetual insecurity and conflict, a struggle for survival in their yearned for safe haven; where once Muslims had been friends, now they were potential enemies of the state. It was deeply disturbing, this constant "suspicion of the stranger, the dark face" as Babu had put it.

Bezalel nodded avidly in agreement. He had always had happy relations with the Muslims during his life in Kerala. After all, Chennamangalam was a city which represented religious harmony. Yet he had left behind the life of that village and Kerala and here he fervently believed that his primary duty was to protect his new country from potential enemies. In India the Muslims had been friends, in Israel it was necessary to defend oneself. Bezalel was an unapologetic realist.

It was a massive mental adjustment, yet he had readily made the sacrifice, jettisoning the old ways. In India he had been a simple villager, a man of peace. Yet in Israel, he had fought in two wars for his new country, in 1967 and then in 1973. Every chance to prove oneself was relished even though he had no prior knowledge or experience of conflict. A fervent Zionist, he chose to push himself to the limit, to do more, not less; to take on the riskiest of enterprises. As a soldier, he had no compunction about tackling Muslim soldiers from Israel's border enemies. His was the pragmatism of a natural warrior, whether in business or battle.

"When we were first training in the army I was asked which group I wanted to join. I chose mine clearance," he said in a quiet determined voice, stripped of conceit or emotion, as if relaying the bare facts. "Our officer said to us 'You're the only people who'll never make a second mistake'. I liked that. I served almost fourteen years. Now my children have all been officers in the army. This is part of the life of Israel."

For him war became his normality and it forged bonds with his fellow Israelis in a way that could never be broken. He learned the nature of Israel during his service. "When you're serving your time, in that group you have a bank manager, a professor, a doctor, a road sweeping man. Everybody together. We eat together, we sleep together, living as one for those days. All backgrounds, all colors, all different types of Jew.

"Everybody knew we had no second choice, we must fight for our survival. That doesn't just mean fight with gun, it means fight to be the best at business, the best at sport, to struggle for the nation. Otherwise we can't survive. Everybody felt we had to come together. We had a feeling: it doesn't matter if we work ten, twelve, fourteen hours a day. It doesn't matter because we're building."

He helped build his nation in many guises: shepherd, soldier, forester and road maintenance man. But his big idea, his real contribution was not in war but helping to build the peace. "Once we had success, many people came to visit us here. The first were two famous French philosophers. What was the name? They came to study us, to find out if there was any problem with color and Indians in Israel. But there was no racism, nothing *I* felt."

Yet he mentioned that sometimes his children were teased at school because of their dark coloring. He took it in his stride. "When they went to school, one time my second son was crying because all the other children called him 'Nigger or negro or black, black, black'. Then we told him *why* we are black. That way they understood. Then later, all the important personalities, ministers, even prime ministers came here to see our farm because we took the lead in that."

In 1994 he received the highest accolade of all. Prime Minister Yitzhak Rabin awarded Bezalel the Kaplan prize for his work in agriculture. The Indian ambassador attended and hosted a party in his honor and told Bezalel his work had given Indians in Israel a good name. But a further honor was to come. At the end of 2005 as Bezalel was receiving radiation treatment for his prostate cancer he received a call from the Indian ambassador.

"Three days before finishing my radiation, I was traveling every day to the hospital in Jerusalem. At this time, the ambassador called me and said 'stop the car and talk with me'. I said 'What happened?'

"He said, 'You've been awarded the Pravasi Bharti Diwas award and you must fly in five days to Hyderabad to get the award from the President of India in January.'

"When I returned, I went to my professor who was treating me and I told him I had to fly. He said, 'On the last day, come early and at eight o'clock we will give you radiation, then come back at four o'clock we'll give second radiation.' The next day he checked me and said I could fly. I went with my wife to the function."

He showed me the award which was framed and hung on his wall of memories. It was signed by President Abdul Kalam, India's Muslim head of state, and bore the crest of three lions. He stroked the crest with his forefinger very gently.

"I was chosen from Indians all over the world. Eleven of us were chosen for this. Two thousand Indians came from all over the world for the function. The others awarded were very big businessmen, from places like the United States. I felt like a fly between these elephants."

I asked if he felt it had been his destiny to come to Israel to achieve all this, that his life may not have been so enriched had he stayed in Cochin. He laughed. "Oh, I don't know," then he thought a bit.

"See, I think I had a nice circle of life," he continued. "That means I started something which brought good things for Israel, good things for India. Now maybe in my next trip to Kerala, to Chennamangalam, I'll try to find people to develop tourism in my village. Because Chennamangalam has a speciality. In 1987 I was invited to Washington by the North American Jewish Flower Growers Association. There I had to give a lecture about my life in India and then in Israel. Then I explained about Chennamangalam."

"Chennamangalam is the only place, maybe in the world, where four religions stay together. That means Jew, Muslim, Hindu and Christian. Each has its specialty. The Hindu worshippers blow the conch shell on festivals, the Muslims call 'Allahu Akhbar', the Jews call with *shofar* and the Christians with bell. Once every seven or eight years, the festivals come at the same time and when this time comes, you can hear them together:

you can hear the conch shell, you can hear the bell, you can hear the shofar and the call of the mosque. Everything. *This* happens only in Chennamangalam. There is nowhere else in the world. Not even in Jerusalem,
which has only three."

The new ambition of the old man who brought roses to Israel's
desert landscape was to disseminate that message of religious unity, a
message that Kerala had instilled in him, to a wider audience.

"Do you miss Kerala ever?"

"No, truly," he lightly touched his heart, then took a slice of Golan
apple and bit into it as he considered his choice. "Kerala is nice to travel
and enjoy. But not for living. Because there's no adventurous life there.
Here, every day we have *the challenge*. Every day we have fight, struggle,
murder, problems. That makes a big difference. Kerala is a calm, cool,
quiet place. Israel is our struggle for survival."

* * * *

Bezalel was one example of a Cochini Jew who had made Israel work for
his family. Yet there were others. After Shahar I went to a place called "Little India" to meet Isaac Chaim Nehemia, who was one of the most senior
Cochini Jewish elders and a leader of the Indian Jews in Israel. He lived in
Nevatim, the biggest Cochini settlement in the country which lay south-
east of Be'er Sheva. Here, 120 Cochini families and 600 people had settled.

Nevatim was, perhaps, the most developed of the *moshavs* where the
Cochinis had settled. It had its own Kerala style synagogue, a museum on
the old history and it observed the faith in the traditional Indian Jewish
manner. In terms of sheer numbers, it was very successful, although less

prosperous than its small neighbor Shahar. As we drove into the *moshav*, the temperature was beginning to drop. In a few hours, the chill of desert evening skies would be with us. Nevatim had none of the regulated perfection of Shahar: the houses looked less fancy and more run down, the gardens and communal areas were not as green and pristine, with lawns overgrown and slightly brown. All around the red desert plains closed in on us, like a sleeping sea, with the mountain ranges of the Jordan beyond.

Disused greenhouses lay abandoned here and there. Like Shahar, Nevatim had suffered a collapse in its flower export business due to competition from African farmers. So many of its residents now worked in Be'er Sheva in regular day jobs, abandoning the land that has begun to retreat to its natural state.

But Nevatim remained a clean and friendly neighborhood. Cochini Jews walked their dogs, children played on the streets safely and everyone seemed happy to help a stranger. Old women tended their gardens or sat in wicker chairs watching the desert skyline change color. A middle aged matron speed walked down the main high road, ample, ghee-upholstered buttocks jostling inside tight sweatpants. Some of the older generation adopted a fusion Indian-Israeli frontier style of dressing— one lady wore her silky *salwar kameez* under a zipped up fleece jacket, while another old man lounged in his garden in a wooly jumper pulled over the *lunghi*, supplemented with woolly socks and Nike trainers. The local children were unmistakably Cochini. One girl aged about eight stopped skipping with her friends and turned slowly to watch our car as we parked to find our bearings. A curtain of dark curly hair fell over one eye as she looked over her shoulder to scrutinize us; her skin was glossy, almost as black as the teak of Kerala, and her eyes the color of molasses.

Youngsters like the girl still celebrated the Jewish festivals the Kerala way, they ate Cochini food, they retained unmistakable south Indian features and yet most had never seen India. Hebrew, not Malayalam, is spoken here and the young are marrying non-Cochini and even non-Indian Jews. It is accepted that Cochini-only marriages are inevitably becoming a thing of the past, even in Nevatim. Slowly, the old Cochin life was being diluted, absorbed into the pan-Israeli national identity that is needed in order to keep the state strong.

Yet I was impressed it had lasted thus far. After fifty years, Cochin remains very much alive in Israel. I was to meet a man who had already succeeded in building the first Cochini synagogue in Israel, the first Cochini museum. Now he wanted to turn Nevatim into a tourist destination for the south, branding it as a Little India. His daughter Nili, a feisty young woman who took tours of the museum, helped her mother Miriam run a Jewish Indian catering business. All of these showed that the Cochini dream was not dying, merely evolving.

I turned up at Isaac Nehemia's house mid afternoon. His house was one of the biggest in the *moshav*: simple, modern and whitewashed, with an adjoining garage large enough for a fleet of cars. Inside, it was full of homely touches and clean lines: white stone floors, white walls and blinds at the windows. All the other rooms led off a large central living area, with a dining room and seating area with plump leather sofas and a massive television. The kitchen led off towards the back of the house, exuding enticing smells of curry and chutneys.

Isaac was a wonderful character, a blend of the Israeli and Indian Jew: loud, gregarious, irrepressible, funny and captivating. He wore a casual brown shirt, with rolled up sleeves and open neck. On his bald head he wore a skullcap made of cotton fabric printed with bright tropical palm leaves, as if in tribute to his old motherland. His eyes shone with child-like delight and when he spoke in his booming baritone it was like listening to a roaring river. His conversation would twist and turn with boundless energy, catching you in its momentum and carrying you along, leaving you happily exhausted by the ride. At the end of a particularly satisfying anecdote, he would throw his head back and laugh with delight, slamming the table with the edge of his fist. There was no reserve, nor artful modesty with this man. He had the brash directness of the Israelis softened by an Indian's emotional warmth. Like his daughter, his smile was enchanting. What God had taken away from Isaac in the hair department, He made up for by way of teeth. Isaac's smile was a joy to behold.

The two were very close and the father evidently loved teasing his daughter. She in turn adored his stories, even though she had clearly heard them so many times before. Very quickly, I felt as if I'd known these two forever. Nili was born in Israel with her five brothers. Her parents had come when they were still small children. Nevatim started off as a small Jewish settlement in 1946, before the formation of Israel. Isaac and his family came in 1954.

The Negev had once been populated by Arabs and particularly the Bedouins. Nomadic tribes living in the desert dated back to the time of the Prophet Abraham himself. Today the Bedouins still have a market, which takes place every Thursday in the southern part of Be'er Sheva, where they trade camels, sheep and goats. Yet it has become more of a show for the tourists, with some of the tribe selling crafts to earn extra income. Given their tradition in the desert, many Jewish families who settled here believed they were safeguarding the land for their own people, said Nili. "The Jewish population in the Negev was isolated and it was mostly Arab around here, so they wanted to protect this area which is where Israel would be. There were eleven settlements like this, one was *moshav* Nevatim, but we the Jewish of Cochin only came in 1954."

They followed another group of Jews who had failed to settle here successfully. They did not know who these people were, merely that the life in the desert had not suited the others. The Cochinis were the next group of immigrants to take up the challenge of desert life. Isaac was just thirteen when he arrived with his parents. Like Bezalel he remembered it as a bleak place. But he was still a child and found the prospect of living in such a place to be intolerable.

"There was nothing, no plants, just dry, dry land. I looked at the desert and cried. I told my mother, 'Why you come here? Why we leave Kerala? Kerala is a very beautiful place'." He reenacted the scene of Isaac the boy, full of tears and horror at the new homeland, weeping and tugging his mother's arm.

"But, my mother said: 'Son, listen. This is the place Abraham started and built the presence in Israel long ago. Great history is here. Be'er Sheva is the start for the Jewish people. If we start working, this place will be our paradise'."

His mother was the dominant force in the family and very religious. His grandfather Abraham Nehemia had been one of the elders in the Thekumbhagam synagogue in Ernakulam. They had decided to come after a man from the Jewish Agency visited Cochin in 1949 to talk to the community about Israel. "He told us 'Israel is now independent, we want Israelis from all over the world to come, Cochin Jews please come.'

We said 'Yes'." He guffawed with laughter, "*Yeees*, we said, because this is our Israel."

His mother called the shots in their household. When he asked her why she had wanted to come here she told the young boy they came to build a homeland. "She said, 'We will work the land and if we work the land it'll give us everything.' Our Torah said Israel is the land of milk and honey. We believed our country would provide for us. Everything we grow here will be successful."

At first it was not so. The first effort to grow crops failed. The *moshav* had seventy-two families then and they seemed set to fail. Then some of the younger generation took specialist agricultural studies, including Isaac. After leaving the army, he returned to form a plan to make the *moshav* work. The plan involved planting vegetables, fruits and rearing chickens. Not everyone could make it work. It was tough and around fifty percent of the original settlers abandoned it for the north.

It was 1961 when Isaac began to put his plan into action. The community planted fruit trees such as apricots and peaches. "These fruits need cool weather but in the spring time, when it makes the fruit, it needs hot weather during day and coolness at nighttime. I said this tree you must plant here. It was success. Yeeah!"

"When we started, this was the weakest *moshav* and within a few years it was one of the most successful economically." From fruit trees, they went into flowers like Shahar and soon Nevatim was also exporting to Europe and earning a good income. In 1964, he married a Cochini Jew who was born in Bombay. Miriam and Isaac had six children.

The *moshav* grew alongside its income until it was the biggest Cochini settlement in Israel. Then the 1984 war hit and like many others, the *moshav's* business slumped. Isaac knew everything had changed. "I told the people of Nevatim, it's finished."

But he was not beaten yet. He had another plan and this one entailed drawing upon the Kerala history. "My community has a big history, a great history. I want to make a reminder of it here," he told me. He was in his late sixties and it would be his last big project, a legacy of sorts. He began some years ago by taking an architect from Israel to Cochin to see the synagogues there. Then a replica was built in his community.

Miriam and her daughter also did their part by running a kitchen that catered to Israelis and foreigners. Earlier that day they had given thirty tourists a breakfast of *idli* and *sambal* for breakfast. Miriam brought out leftovers for us to try. Tourism was to be Nevatim's future. Already, Isaac was marking out a vision which comprised new roads, water pumps, enhanced sewage systems, to prepare for the coming of the tourists. He wanted to build an Indian culture theater and host conferences and meetings here. I wasn't sure whether it would happen, after all it sounded like a costly investment and where would the money come from? But Isaac was undeterred by the practicalities. He had his vision and it would become real.

"I see a small Kerala here. We want to show people our canals, the water, the fishnets of Cochin," he told me as his great hands conjured visions of the future, mapped upon his kitchen table. His Tropicana *kippah* had slipped down in his excitement and he readjusted it.

I asked how his people had settled here among other Israelis and he explained that many were now marrying non-Indian Jews. There was a better understanding of the great depth of history and culture of their people. This instilled a natural sense of self-worth, said Nili. "I can say in

Israel, the Cochin Jewry was successful in immigration. We don't suffer from feeling we're lower than other Israelis."

Yet it was evident that color continued to be an issue at times in Israel as well. Their neighbors, the Ethiopian Jews, felt it and drew comfort from the Cochinis, who seemed incredibly self-assured despite their coloring. The source of the Cochini Jews' self-assurance was, perhaps, their history.

"We left India as a very proud people and we're still a very proud people here," Nili explained. "Even the younger generation who've entered mixed marriages, they say, 'I am Cochini.' They're still proud. Nobody can say to me 'You are less than me'. Some Ethiopian Israelis used to ask me: 'How come you don't feel less in Israel, because you're dark?' I said to them, 'First of all I have a beautiful color. I am chocolate and everyone wants our color, you know.' Here, we have an Ashkenazim school, and they're all white. On friendly days they say to us, 'You have a beautiful color.' Then when they want to tease us, they say 'Oh, you are dark like chocolate.' I say to them 'And you are cheese. Cheese is less tasty than chocolate'." She smiled at her story and glanced at her father for approval.

Then she added more seriously that sometimes the issue of color evoked the old Cochini divide. "One Ashkenazim said to me in the museum, 'You're not Jewish because you're black.' I said: 'Abraham was a dark man was he not? Not blue eyed and blond.' All of his friends told me I was right. And I told him, 'Now you need to ask yourself who you are'."

However proud she was of her Jewish Indian culture and however bold she was in defending it, Nili acknowledged it would be difficult to preserve as so many Kerala Jews were marrying outsiders within Israel.

She remained optimistic for her own fortunes, all the same, telling me if she could not find a Cochini man to marry, then she would marry an outsider and instill in her husband the Kerala ways. I had no doubt of it, for behind her father's smile lay her grandmother's indomitable will.

"It's what I want. It's in my blood," she said firmly, running her fingers through her bobbed hair. "It's never going away, no matter who I marry. See, my aunty married an Ashkenazi. He told her 'Wife, I will never eat spice'. Every Shabbat she would lovingly make her spiciest chicken dish from Cochin. Every Shabbat he would refuse. After so many refusals, on so many Shabbats, he now eats the same food. He even asks for this one dish. *This* will be my way also."

* * * *

It was night by the time I left Nevatim. The desert was cold and empty again as we climbed into the car to leave the father and daughter on the threshold, waving their goodbyes. They had shown me their community, replete with a gaily painted replica of the Ernakulam synagogue and the museum. After fifty years, the Cochini Jewish way of life was thriving in the Middle East just as it was dying in southern India. The community here took every opportunity to push things forward to the next generation. They were ruthless in their pragmatism as one would expect of a desert people. If they could not marry a Cochini, then they would marry another Jew and show them the Kerala Jewish life. It was better than the alternative.

My thoughts settled on Nili and her good humored determination to make her future husband love Cochin as much as he loved her. She was very much the modern Israeli woman and yet despite having never stepped foot in Cochin, she was unmistakably a daughter of Kerala. I remembered Anil Abraham's ardent wish as he played with the peppercorn necklace beside the riverbank near Parul. Here was one Jewish girl who would not give him headaches.

As Nazeeh and I drove away, heading back to Jerusalem, I considered these remarkable stories of adaptation. The elders had plucked whole communities from the tropics and transplanted them to the desert. The motivation of the people I had met so far had been Zionism, to follow in the footsteps of Abraham and take on the toughest of assignments by bringing a Jewish renewal to the Negev. The differences between what they sacrificed and what they embraced were marked not just by the contrasting landscapes, but equally in the religious mentality of the Jewish communities in India and Israel. Kerala offered a conservative, highly traditional and orthodox way of life for the Jews. Israel was the Jewish homeland and yet it was fast paced, modern and secular. Even Isaac had noted the difference when he first arrived as a small boy, telling me that he was shocked to see people working on Shabbat, to see that not every community had a synagogue by way of right. In Westernized secular Israel, the synagogue was not the absolute center of life as it was in rural Kerala.

I was driving beneath a canopy of velvet blue skies on the road toward the Holy City that remained the heartbeat of the faith which sustained the body of the Jewish people even in their long exile and dispersal. Always, day or night, when traveling through these lands, past signposts that were not merely traffic directions but markers of history, one was overwhelmed by the past. This was more true in Jerusalem than any other place I had ever seen. In the morning, I would meet a man who had come to Israel more than thirty years ago. Not for Zionism, for he was not a politically minded man, nor was he a man who sought economic opportunity or freedom from Kerala. Abraham Eliavoo had come to Israel more than thirty years ago for the love of his faith. He had come to immerse himself in the history of his people and to be part of the ultimate religious experience of living in the Holy City. Being a religious man he had seen it as his duty to leave behind the privilege and comfort of his village in India to end his life in the city of Solomon. He lived with his family here, he worked for the good of the nation and prayed regularly at the Western Wall, which continued to hold the power to move him to tears even now. The dream had been realized. And yet all was not well in Jerusalem.

* * * *

CHAPTER TWELVE

Home

*"So when God destroyed the cities of the plain, He remembered
Abraham, and He brought Lot out of the catastrophe that overthrew
the cities where Lot had lived."*

—GENESIS 19:29

It was five o'clock in the morning and most of Jerusalem was sleeping. Abraham awoke for prayers. His body was stiff from cold and his bad leg always proved more resistant to movement at this time. He reached out for his stick and hauled himself onto his feet. After prayers, he ate breakfast and prepared to leave for work as an accountant at the Star of David emergency services organization in the center of town. He had to be out of the house by six thirty in order to catch the bus on time. His working day began at seven thirty in the morning through to three in the afternoon, six days a week. Afterwards, he would go to the local shopping mart and pick up some provisions before taking the bus home. After making his way up the steep pathway and steps, he finally reached the house and let himself in. There, he would prepare a cup of tea, not proper Indian *chai* which was boiled in a pan with milk, sugar and black leaves, but the inadequate sort made with a bag dipped in hot water.

Afterward, he would make something to eat and await the family's return at night.

It would be a grueling routine for a young man in his prime, but Abraham was seventy-eight and unable to walk without the aid of his stout stick. He had lost his sense of optimism long ago, yet he retained the fierce independence of the young man who moved to Israel more than three decades ago. His routine, which began at five and ended late into the night, was the price Abraham had to pay to live in the Holy City. In India, he had a life of privilege, education, money and servants. Here, he could not afford to retire or hire help.

It was not that he had not worked hard. Nor that he had no family to hand. Abraham had grafted all his life and yet still could not muster enough of a pension to retire. He lived with his second son and family in one of Jerusalem's better suburbs in a modern house with a small garden. From the living room one could see a dramatic panorama of the city. A concrete ring of tower blocks nestled in the hills surrounding the old city, a modern-day fortress to keep out the enemy. Within the next concentric circle lay the newer part of the city, with the emblems of the nation state: opulent hotels, grand museums, government buildings and the Knesset nestling within. At the very heart was the eternal city of gold, Old Jerusalem. From a great distance, the pearl-like shimmer of the Western Wall concourse can be visible on a clear day, sitting alongside the iridescent majesty of the Dome of the Rock. After all the incantations of longing to go to Jerusalem one day, now Abraham could gaze upon it every morning from his window, taking in the millennial sweep of history over a cup of tea. From a distance it seemed perfect, the dream realized and everything he hoped it would be. But as the brutal reality of everyday existence zeroed in, life in the Holy City was one of long working hours, high taxes, a crippling cost of living and fear.

Culturally, it was very different from the Jewish way of life in India. Here, society was fast, highly modern and Westernized, with Israeli society taking many of its cues from the United States. Religion sometimes seemed to take a secondary place to survival in the lives of many ordinary busy Israelis, even while lying at the very heart of the country's political troubles.

When Abraham and his family had chosen to make the *aliyah* they saw it as a spiritual homecoming. The weight of expectation was so great after two thousand years of exile that it was bound to end in anti-climax. He fully expected faith to be at the center of everything, much as it was in Jew Town in Kerala. There, religion permeated every facet of daily life, whether a person was Hindu, Muslim, Christian, Sikh or Jewish. The village pace of life made it easier to accommodate God and ritual into everyday existence. There, life had been financially easier as well. Living in Israel meant having to work longer hours to pay higher bills, which meant that a lot of people could not afford to even respect Sabbath in this, the Holy Land.

But most of all, Kerala had afforded him a peace of mind. Co-existence was not an aim for ideal times, but simply the way there. The Jew would invite the Muslim into his home as a trusted friend. The Muslim would bring sweets to the Jew when he broke his fast during Ramadan, sharing his blessings. In Jerusalem, for the first time in his life Abraham had to rewire this logic and go against his natural instincts to live in a city where a Muslim brother, whether Palestinian or any other nationality, equated fear.

I first met Abraham at his office on Hamag Street in central Jerusalem. It was a modern building with an outpatient section in the foyer. An armed security guard, a Somali Jew, manned the entrance and scanned the bodies and bags of all who entered for traces of explosive. He did it as if it were no big deal, rather like asking visitors to put on an ID badge. This was routine procedure in the city which had until recently been targeted by waves of suicide bombers after the beginning of the second *intifada*.

* * * *

Abraham's office was positioned at the end of a corridor to the right of the foyer. He stood up to greet me, a dark skinned man with kindly eyes screened behind thick glasses and the familiar Indian paunch protruding beneath his jumper. A small white knitted *kippah* covered his bald head, framed by a halo of fine silvery hair. He wore a shirt and thick ribbed brown sweater pulled tight over his belly and grey slacks. He had a ready smile with neat even teeth. Seeing I was an Indian, his face was animated with evident delight.

Abraham spoke in soft, precise cadences, emanating a kindly wisdom like Yoda from *Star Wars*. He offered a chair and immediately made arrangements for coffee to be served, diligent in his duties as the host. He seemed particularly concerned I was not taking sugar and personally tore open a sachet and poured its contents into my cup, as if worried that I should miss out on a treat. Seeing I was comfortable, he settled back into the administrative chaos of his small empire. A cassette-player tinkled Bollywood music in the background, the notes of its jangling melodies floated through the open window like pollen into the courtyard garden below.

Every bit of available space on his desk was covered in piles of medical correspondence: claims, follow-up paperwork, sets of accounts, plus great bundles of unopened letters that still had to be sifted and sorted. Abraham sat with his hands folded in his lap, still and calm amid this paper storm. It was a throwback to every Indian office I had ever visited: a mysterious, unfathomable Eastern order concealed amidst the pandemonium of towers of brown files, paperwork and half-eaten *pakoras*.

He reminded me very much of his first grandchild Anil, whom I met in Cochin. Anil clearly held a cherished spot in his grandfather's affections and remained at the foremost of his thoughts and prayers. More than anyone in his family, Abraham worried for his grandson's future and his marriage prospects in particular. It was to become a recurring theme in our conversations: the need for Anil to find a Jewish wife.

He told me his family was from Ernakulam where he had once managed a construction business. There he had been a wealthy man with land and property and good connections from his days as a senior member of the ruling Communist Party. He dabbled in politics and even considered a political career, but decided to forsake all that for the chance to come to Israel. For his family, Israel was not a matter of choice, but of faith.

But having returned "home", Abraham found the Jewish observances were often ignored in this modern, secular nation. The pace of life was faster, more expensive, less bound by tradition. In his late seventies, he found himself living the eternal dream in the Holy Land, yet somehow the spiritual moorings of his life had been loosened. Now after thirty years, he was thinking of returning to India.

"After I came here, after six months I saw this place is no good for me, I want to return back to Cochin," he told me, his small head wobbling in anxiety. "Unfortunately, we sold all the properties there. So many times I tried to go back to Cochin. But I found I could not, for some reason or another. Now on the tenth of January, I'm going. Not for holiday. Maybe I'll never come back."

I asked him why he was leaving Jerusalem now, after so much and after so long? The city meant everything to him. It had been worth losing India for thirty years.

"Jerusalem!" He sighed, twiddling the volume control on his tape recorder as he turned up a hit he particularly favored. "If you come one time, it *is* paradise. But to stay . . ." His voice trailed off sadly, cheeks puffed out in dismay like a sad child. "In Cochin there was no trouble, there was no trouble for Jews. Here, it's a different story. Yesterday, you asked me to meet you there, at your residence (I was staying at the Notre Dame guesthouse just outside the old city walls). I couldn't come *there*. We're *afraid* to come there, near East Jerusalem. They're dragging people, shooting people."

"You go to the Wailing Wall?" I asked.

"Wailing Wall, I'm going. But I'm taking the bus number two from here and *just* going to the Wailing Wall. When I'm before the Wall, I feel I'm standing before heaven." He paused as he briefly journeyed into his memories before coming back to me again. "Then I return home by bus," he said. "The Wall is safe, the bus is safe."

But Israel generally was not, he believed. I was to find out that Abraham had suffered an internal struggle for some time. On the one hand, in this city he believed he was closer to God. He marveled that he was lucky enough to be able to visit the Wall but not as frequently as he would wish. Whenever he did go, it comforted him and compensated for all he had relinquished. He had fulfilled the religious duty to return to the Holy Land. But three decades on, it was not enough. Israel failed to fill the emotional and spiritual vacuum in his heart after he left India. He was saddened to see the lack of religious observance in the Holy Land, he felt neglectful of his own duties as a Jew because he was too busy working and prayed less than he did in Cochin. He saw how modern ways were taking his own family further away from the traditions of the faith that had ruled their lives in Cochin. Last, the political violence corrupted his peace of mind. He was still a man of the village. He remembered how Jew, Muslim and Christian had lived as friends and neighbors and in this new life he could not reconcile the clash between the ethos of his faith and culture and the political cost of realizing the dream of the Promised Land.

Abraham's eldest son Sam, Anil and Solomon's father, had also come out to Israel with the family in 1971. Abraham and his wife followed two years later with their parents. Initially, they were all flushed with optimism at the thought of resettling here. With his skills as a manager for a major construction company in Kerala, he felt he had something valuable to contribute to a country which needed to build itself from scratch. The construction dream never materialized. Also, in the end, Sam and his family were defeated by the violence and siege like atmosphere that was part of Israel.

After Sam's arrival, war broke out in 1973. In October that year Egypt and Syria launched an attack on Israel. It was the date of Yom Kippur. Sam fought in that war and then again in the 1984 war with

Lebanon. He was a tank driver and saw action on the front line. He did not wish to resurrect the experience. The wars marked him deeply. Unlike Bezalel, he could not reconcile himself to the violence which was so against everything he had ever known in India. It helped him to decide to leave and return to Kerala.

"He got the shock from the war," Abraham explained. "We all did. My wife became ill and then in 1985 she expired. Sam also suffered deeply from his mother's death and that was it. He decided to go back to Cochin."

Anil had told me in Cochin that his father rarely spoke of those days of conflict in 1973 and 1984. He felt uneasy fighting against men who looked much like those he had grown up alongside in India, men who were not so different from old friends. He fulfilled his duty to his country, but he was not a fighting man. He did not want this for his sons who were still very young, so the family went home. Abraham told me the fear of those terror-stricken days of Israel being destroyed had passed. Yet the internal security menace remained ever present.

"We're still afraid because of the security situation. All the places for Jews have security. Even here you've seen the security guard. In India, Jews had a very peaceful existence. In Ernakulam we were surrounded by so many people of different religions. On Jew Street we had one mosque and two synagogues. Yet we saw had no trouble with our neighbors.

"Why do I think of going home? I'm an old man. I wish to have peace, to pray in peace. In Cochin there was no tension. No tension," he emphasized, lifting his hands to the skies and letting them fall again. "In all the places where we lived—Cochin, Chennamangalam, Parul— no tension."

Even as he spoke of no tension, I could feel his tension. And little wonder. Earlier that year there had been a brief but brutal skirmish. Israel's northern settlements had faced rock launcher bombardment from Lebanon, incurring an Israeli retaliation with all its formidable firepower. Yet this bloody confrontation, which the world watched in dismay, was less of an immediate concern to Abraham than the ceaseless paranoia of suicide bombings in the city where he lived. This was the "tension" he spoke of: the crippling dread of an invisible enemy, an enemy who might even look like your friend, who could blow up a bus, a car or a marketplace at any time.

"For now, Jerusalem's more calm," he told me. "But for how long? Before, each month, each week there were explosions of suicide bombs in Jerusalem. *Every* week. Every week from 2003 to 2005, every week there was news of a suicide bombing. So many Israelis died."

He compared this to India, where there was no history of Jews being targeted by fanatics, despite India being home to one of the largest Muslim communities in the world. The synagogue resided next to the police station in Mattancherry, yet the threat was deemed so miniscule that I rarely saw the police officer awake at his post. There, of course, the situation was very different. The Jews had been such a tiny minority group that they did not register on the political radar of militant religious groups from either Hinduism or Islam. There they were not power brokers. Here, the Kerala Jews had to wake up to a relentless struggle for their survival. After thirty years, Abraham was tired of struggling.

* * * *

The next day was Shabbat, so Abraham would spend his day at the local synagogue. On Sunday he worked as usual until three. He told me that he had not visited the Wall for six months. He was put off by the journey and the security fears, so I offered to pick him up from work and go there with him. He seemed pleased with the suggestion and agreed.

He told me that for all Jews the Wall represented sacrifices. After the destruction of the Second Temple almost two thousand years before, the only remaining part was the Western Wall. The ancient Jews had sacrificed their lives to protect it. Today it was a place to remember, a place to supplicate before God.

He issued me with instructions ahead of our visit, already excited. "The first time people visit they feel they can bring their problems here. Even Hillary Clinton came and put her paper in the wall. You can put your request to God in this place and here you will receive the answer."

One could imagine what Hillary had asked for. Abraham told me I should also write a petition to place in the Wall. He told me the Wall was the only reason he came to Israel. It was the reason he had stayed so long. I asked him if he had ever offered a petition at the Wall. "Only twice. Both times, He answered," he replied.

On Sunday afternoon I picked him up in the car. The Palestinian driver Nazeeh decided he would use the journey as an opportunity to ask how he could get a job as an ambulance driver as tourism earnings had collapsed since the conflict with Lebanon. The two dipped in and out of Hebrew and English. Abraham told Nazeeh that the rules were very strict, that one would need a clean driving license for at least two years—that meant no tickets, no accidents. This set the usually mild-mannered Nazeeh off. He launched into a tirade about the iniquity of such a requirement. As he turned around to me to protest, averting all attention from the traffic flow, he shouted, "It is *impossible*. Show me a driver in Jerusalem with no tickets and I show you a man who does not drive. Two years is too long. And you're telling me I must have no accidents in this time? Can you believe this?" he now gestured to me in the rear mirror.

"The job's for an ambulance driver. Is it unreasonable to expect a driver who does not cause accidents?" I replied.

"Perhaps," he shrugged. "But for Israeli, I am sure there is no problem getting through this paperwork. For Palestinian, always extra demands, bigger headaches. Still, I will try. The old man says what to lose, eh?"

The old Jew and the young Palestinian seemed to get on well. At one stage they became engrossed in an amusing conversation in Hebrew and laughed uproariously. When asked what they were discussing, Nazeeh looked sheepish and replied untruthfully, "Don't worry. It's not so interesting."

We arrived at the entrance by Dung Gate at 3:30 PM, near the car park. The huge plaza that stands before the vast Western Wall is accessed only through a high security checkpoint—an airport style walk-through screener to detect weapons or explosive, plus a bag check by Israeli officers. Abraham fished into his bag and gave me a cream silk headscarf to cover the head before going to the Wall. The plaza was thronging with people. There were few tourists, mostly Jewish families.

The Wall towered before us. The vast structure was built of huge pale gold slabs of Jerusalem stone, some of which were two meters high. In its time, the Second Temple had been a vision of God's glory on earth.

The walls were adorned with white marble delicately veined with lines of red and blue. The ancient Jewish historian Flavius Josephus describes doors of gold leading into the Hekhal which were further embellished with "golden vines from which depended grape clusters as tall as a man". A curtain of scarlet, blue and purple linen and embroidered with sun, moon and stars hung above the doors.

Josephus described the Temple's supporting walls as "the greatest ever heard of". The longest of them was the western wall, which measured 530 yards. The stones used for these walls were massive, with some weighing as much as five tons. The sanctuary of the Temple was gilded and from a distance the building was an ethereal vision of white and gold, dazzling onlookers in the sunlight, as if Yahweh himself had blinded them with his presence for a moment.

Abraham headed towards the men's section of the Wall, while I went to the women's on the right. The approach was down a steep path that led directly to the bare stone. White plastic chairs were sporadically set out to allow people to sit and pray, contemplate or just rest. Low level wooden lecterns stood ready with copies of the Torah.

The women, heads covered in squares of silk, lined up in rows against the Wall, some gently rocking side to side while holding their arms across their chests, others with heads bobbing back and forth, their faces pressed up against the bare stone. Here the Jews come to commune directly with God. Several of the women were weeping, wet cheeks pressed against the pages of the open Torah, forehead and bodies leaning into the Wall as they sobbed their sorrows and entreaties into the sun-warmed stone. Tears coursed down the cheeks of many of the women who prayed here, from old orthodox Jews, dressed head to toe in black with thick dark stockings and sensible shoes to young mothers rocking their toddlers or swaddled newborn in their arms. There were young female Israeli soldiers, their carelessly slung rifles in arresting contrast to their demure and pious demeanor. I watched one beautiful young Jewess, silky black hair swathed in a pink scarf of roses that framed her perfectly made up face as she bowed her head in prayer, rocking on her black stiletto boots, arms wrapped tight around her white fake fur jacket.

They came. Young and old, black and white. There was no sound discernable apart from the weeping and murmur of passages of the Torah. Lovebirds, sleek with chests blushing a soft pink swooped overhead and settled into cracks in the wall high over our heads, watching the people below. Tiny sparrows whizzed over our heads and burrowed into the gaps to feed their chicks. The lower cracks and crevices between the huge slabs of stone were jammed with countless scraps of white paper, each one containing a personal epistle.

Some of the pilgrims were so overwhelmed they simply fell prostrate at the foot of the Wall itself. Time passed quickly as I sat and watched the tide of people. They shed tears in a way I had rarely seen, even at other significant places of pilgrimage for other faiths. Why did they cry so? Was it for themselves? Was it a sudden realization of the pain suffered by their people over the millennia, or did they cry for the burden of their history which continued to deny them peace, even here in the Promised Land? It was a place to unload the agonies of past and present, personal and communal.

When a space cleared, I did as Abraham suggested and placed my own petition amidst the thousands of others, as non-Jews are allowed to do. I left to meet up with him. He was slowly making his way across the plaza, a tiny little figure in a green puffa jacket amid this vast sea of white stone.

"What did you pray for," I asked. "Did you pray to return to India?"

"Not India. I prayed for Anil. My firstborn grandchild. I pray that he finds a good girl to marry. He desires marriage above all else for his happiness. That is all."

"You prayed for a Cochini Jewish girl?"

"Not just Cochini. Those days are gone. *Any* Jewish girl. But she must be soft minded, a good heart. I only ask God, 'Give him a wife who will not give him headache'."

I thought once again of the peppercorn necklace in Anil's pocket. His quest was now in the arena of the highest power.

* * * *

Afterwards, Nazeeh dropped us off at Abraham's house. Inside, he took us through to the kitchen-living room. His fourteen-year-old granddaughter was sprawled on the floor with her friend, television blaring, as they roared with laughter at an Israeli standup comedian. She barely acknowledged him when he entered, continuing her conversation with her friend as Abraham introduced us and set about making tea and cutting thick slices of cake.

In sharp contrast to the old fashioned courtesy that the young show the old in India, this young girl ignored him, turning up the TV sound to drown her grandfather's voice. He limped about the kitchen, refusing my offer to help and insisting on acting the host, in the Indian way.

The family Chihuahua nipped my shoe and then settled by my feet as I drank tea, eyes fixed on me like black coals smoldering in the snow of his white fur, as if looking for any sign of provocation to attack. As his granddaughter continued to ignore him, guffawing loudly, he repeated emphatically that it was time to leave Jerusalem.

"I see now this isn't for me. My son and grandchildren here are not keeping the Sabbath and festivals. Not because of work, they don't care for our religion. In three decades, I've made the journey from Israel to India nineteen times. I've more feeling for the grandchildren there, you see."

Abraham was surrounded by family in this house. He couldn't move for family. He worked and lived an active life and at last, he was in the land of his forefathers. He prayed at the Wall which seemed to be his only source of comfort in a city that was a stranger. In his first winter in Jerusalem he had experienced snowfall. It measured twenty centimeters high and he remembered the shock of seeing tiny symmetrical icicles in the shape of flowers. At the time it seemed magical and emblematic of his new life which seemed to offer an air of every possibility. Now when he thought of snow, there was no glitter of delight in his eyes. The coldness of snowfalls in Jerusalem merely made him recall the warmth of Cochin. The unobserved Sabbath reminded him of prayers in the houses of friends in Ernakulam. The drudgery of working life here underscored the life of ease he had forsaken. And every time he watched the news to see pictures of carnage and war, he thought of Jew Town, his friends from the synagogue and the mosque and the temple.

"As a young man, when I first came here, I told myself, 'Abraham, this is heaven.' Now I know. *Not* heaven." He broke off a piece of cake, offering it to the dog that licked it up eagerly. Now as he approached his ninth decade, Abraham wanted to overturn his life once more, leave the land of his prophets and make a fresh *aliyah* back to India.

"I am more than seventy. I am in my last years and I think *nothing* of the future," he told me, head wobbling gently from side to side, palms resting flat on his thighs. "I don't worry. I really don't worry any more. I only seek a calm life now, to finish my life with calmness. To *die* in calmness. In Cochin. This is my wish."

* * * *

Later that afternoon after leaving Abraham I walked through Jaffa Gate, one of the vast gateways that lead into the ancient citadel city, and made my way towards the Tower of David. Its pale stonework glowed in the dying sunshine. I bought a ticket and passed through the gates to gardens of blue lavender that filled an old courtyard suffused with its perfume. I mounted the sequence of steep stairwells that led to the viewing platform at the top which afforded uninterrupted views across the rooftops of Old Jerusalem. The sun was descending and hung low now, a mellow orange disc in pale blue skies. The city lay below, an ancient and intricate labyrinth of gold and shadow that had been the source of spiritual inspiration and suffering. I could see tiny figures thronging the narrow walkways below that threaded together the separate quarters of the city.

Each was a microcosm of Jerusalem's heritage, peoples who loved the city and spilled blood for it over the millennia.

In the middle distance was the Temple Mount, the disputed site that is venerated by both Muslims and Jews, and therein the gold glint of the

Dome of the Rock shrine and the silver of El-Aqsa Mosque. The surrounding pathways fed into the heart of the Arab souk in the Muslim quarter, which was congregated with women shopping for provisions, some wearing designer jeans, while others remained cloaked in the anonymity of the *burqa* with just almond kohl eyes visible, a tantalizing glimpse of their masked vivaciousness evident in scarlet painted toe nails. They haggled with the stallholders without pity for profit, selecting the choicest produce, beating down the prices before gathering up their brown-paper parcels to their bosom. There were handsome clean-shaven youths and bearded old men with sun-withered faces of parchment, earnest in conversation as they walked in pairs, sometimes hands lightly linked in friendship as is the Eastern way. Those on their way to the mosque wore prayer caps as they hurried for *namaaz*, attired in immaculate white robes that somehow defied the film of dust that engulfed all else. Others dressed in Arab-style headscarves and expensive *kaftan* robes, their wealth displayed via thick gold rings and bracelets glinting upon fingers and wrists.

Whole lanes were devoted to spices and condiments, others to brass pots and kitchen ware. In the food market, hawkers hollered out prices in Arabic, proffering buyers a taste of olives and dates or sugar-dusted Turkish Delight shot through with slivers of pistachio or flavored with essence of lemon and rose. Pomegranates were sliced open at a whim to reveal creamy insides studded with seeds the color and clarity of rubies in a Pasha's jeweled turban. In the meat quarter, halal butchers brandished fearsome bloodied choppers that deftly sliced stacks of mutton ribs or quartered chickens beneath the unremitting scrutiny of fearsome elderly matriarchs, moustaches bristling at the slightest hint of being cheated.

Along the Via Dolorosa in the Christian quarter, the pathway once taken by Christ as he carried his cross to Calvary is lined now with scores of souvenir shops such as the "Ninth Station Boutique", many of which are run by Christian Palestinians. As one traces the steps of Christ on his path of suffering, one is assailed by the vision of thousands of religious icons, a myriad of gold-leafed halos in resplendent relief. Wall upon wall of crosses, rosaries and scapulas hung in an array of beads and color, baskets of precious vials of holy water from the River Jordan or earth excavated from Bethlehem and entombed in tiny lockets, promising to ward off a manifold of evils. Pavement galleries depicting the Crucifixion, the Last Supper, Mary and baby Jesus stared out at all who passed, as shopkeepers beckoned passing trade with open palms and the Eastern promise of "Very cheap" or "Very antique".

In the lanes that led to the Jewish quarter and Western Wall, the Jews made their way through the uneven warren until they reached the security gates which were protected by armed guards, special walkway scanners and x-ray machines. Orthodox Jews who made Jerusalem their mission, wearing wide brimmed hats and heavy black coats, impervious to the climate; conservative womenfolk in headscarves and wigs grasped tightly the hands of *kippah*-capped children. They skipped quickly towards their destination, as if running late for an appointment, watched by Palestinian shopkeepers whose eyes burned with a thousand suppressed grievances.

From high above the old city, the rushing figures seemed one and the same, a blur of flowing robes in the colors of the landscape itself. The tableau seemed set in a time that was millennia old, beyond modernity. As the shadows deepened, the fragrance of lavender and incense, shaami kebab and fried onion appeased the senses. In the distance the shimmering white concourse of the Western Wall shone still. And beyond lay the majestic Dome of the Rock, marking the site of a black rock where it is believed Muhammad ascended to heaven on his white steed after completing his Night Journey. The Rock is seen by both Muslim and Jew to be "the center of the world, the entrance to the Garden of Eden, source of fertility", said Armstrong's *A History of Jerusalem.* Who holds the key to this sacred gateway remains a source of strife—any threat to this place from one or the other could ignite the whole of Jerusalem once more.

From a distance, all one discerned was beauty and it did not seem possible that stones had the power to make a city bleed. If one sat high above the old city and listened during the course of the day one would discern the peel of bells from the Christian quarter, the haunting cry of the *muezzin* from the Muslim quarter and the triumphal blast of the *shofar.* Yet unlike Kerala, in Jerusalem the sounds spoke of discord not unity.

Surveying the eternal city as it surrendered to night, until all that was visible was the stark silhouette of minarets and domes against purple skies, I remembered earlier that day, after dropping Abraham at his house, Nazeeh told me he had appreciated the old man's manners. It was his city too and yet many Israelis made him feel like he did not belong. He had not felt that with the old man. He was all the more approving when he heard of the Jews' relations with the Muslims in India itself. It was all a revelation to him. In this city where his forefathers had grown up, Nazeeh constantly fretted for the future of his children. Would they have the chance of a good job; would they have a house of their own; or the chance of peace? Last and most worrisome of all, would a place remain for them in their ancestral land? He had no satisfying answers to any of these questions. Some of these questions had also preoccupied the Cochini Jews and compelled many to leave their interim paradise for Israel.

Here, Nazeeh had little optimism for relations between the two warring brothers and pointed to the partition wall that was being constructed at that time along the West Bank, severing the Palestinian community from their source of work, the outside world and their water supply. He believed this effective apartheid was a way of crushing his community's future into the dust.

This division was part of the unease that plagued some of the older Cochini Jews who came to Israel. Some, but not all. The issue of division within the Holy Land itself had not been a cause for concern for the Zionists among them. Whenever we discussed the subject of the Arab-Israeli conflict, men like Bezalel and Isaac viewed the battle for survival as necessary, part of a destiny that had been set out for the Israeli people. It was not for them to question.

Yet others, among the Malabari immigrants in particular, sensed an echo of their own tragedy in the Palestinians. They too knew what it was to be usurped in their historical narrative, to face separation. In Kerala, division had led to destruction. Perhaps their fear was of the cycle repeating itself.

This was all part of the "tension" that Abraham spoke of. His faith was one which was rooted in Judaism as a religion of justice. He remembered that the Jews and Muslims sprang from the same founding father.—the Prophet Abraham. Therefore, theirs was an unnatural enmity.

After so much anticipation and the grievance of the history of the Black and White Jews in Kerala, Abraham, his son Sam and others like

Babu found the just society they had craved, the *shalom* that comes from harmony was absent even in the Holy Land, just as it was once absent in Cochin. Sam and Babu's judgment had been swift: Israel was not home.

It had taken Abraham thirty years to make his decision to leave. In the end he was defeated by a spiritual dislocation and insecurity that was too high a price to pay. In the period that followed my visit, the suicide bombings would worsen, magnifying the nightmare.

His imminent return took the saga of the Kerala Jews full circle. It had begun three thousand years ago in the magnificent fortress city that stretched before me. The Temple, that touchstone of faith was destroyed, and pain resonated to this day in all the Jews who came to the Western Wall. India was meant to be no more than an interim paradise, but two thousand years had made the Jews as much a part of the fabric of India as the Hindu or Muslim or Christian. After nourishing the dream of Jerusalem for millennia, Abraham's generation finally made the joyous pilgrimage home.

Men like Bezalel found their mission completed. It was as if they were whole again. In a remarkable reinvention, they relinquished the past, choosing to renew all that was best from India in the motherland. Their homecoming provided the deliverance of renewal at a time when the old life in Cochin was beyond redemption.

Yet Abraham encountered alienation and sorrow. Sixty years have passed since Indian independence, since the formation of Israel, geopolitical landmarks which ushered in the compulsion for change in the lives of ordinary men and women. After three decades of war and the guerilla warfare of terrorism and counter-terrorism, Abraham remained unable to reconcile faith with conflict. It was true it was over for his people in Kerala. Yet he foresaw his own imminent demise and preferred it to be within the embrace of the past. This desire to return provided an unexpected epitaph, compelling Abraham to find rest in a land that had given the Jews so much, a peace that history has rarely bestowed. In the end it was an age-old tolerance that drew him.

* * * *

ACKNOWLEDGMENTS

Thanks to the people who made this book possible. First, I am fortunate to have publishers who are both inspiring individuals as well as great editors. Thank you to my London publisher Philip Gwyn Jones, publisher of Portobello Books and Granta, and his team, including Laura Barber and Hannah Marshall. Thank you to Brando Skyhorse and his team at Skyhorse Publishing in New York, and to Ravi Singh, publisher at Penguin India in New Delhi. I'm also grateful to freelance editor Daphne Tagg for her insightful copy-editing and to my literary agent Ayesha Karim at Aitken Alexander Associates for her valued support. Thank you to Storm Design for my website: www.ednafernandes.com.

The book was made possible by the kind co-operation of the Cochini Jews of Ernakulam, Mattancherry and Israel. Throughout, I have valued their trust, generosity of spirit in the face of adversity and stories. I am appreciative of the help I received at the British Museum, the Paradesi and Chennamangalam synagogues, as well as the Israel Museum in Jerusalem.

Last, love and thanks to my friends and family, particularly: Felix, Andrew Atkinson, Max and Elfina Fernandes, Maria Fernandes, Tania Fernandes, and Bernard and Sylvia Atkinson.

E.F., 2008

LIST OF REFERENCES

Armstrong, Karen, *A History of Jerusalem*, UK, HarperCollins, 1996

Benjamin, Joshua M., *The Mystery of Israel's Ten Lost Tribes*, India, Mosaic Books, 1989

Book of Baruch, 10

Buchanan, Claudius, *Christian Researches in Asia*, UK, Cadell & Davies, 1812

Correa, Gaspar, *The Three Voyages of Vasco da Gama and His Viceroyalty*, UK. Reprint of an 1968 edition by the Hakluyt Society, London

Diamond, Jared, *Collapse: How Societies Choose to Fail or Survive*, USA, Viking Penguin, 2005

Gandhi, *Book of Quotations*, India, 1931

Genesis 19:29

Goitein, Shlomo D., *A Mediterranean Society: The Jewish Communities of the World as Portrayed in the Cairo Genizah*, US, University of California Press, 1993

Goldberg, David J. and Rayner, John D., *The Jewish People, Their History and Their Religion*, UK, Viking, 1987

Isaiah 11:11

Isaac, I.A., *A Short Account of the Calcutta Jews with a Sketch of the Bene Israels, the Cochin Jews, the Chinese Jews and the Black Jews of Abyssinia*, India, 1917

Jews of Cochin, India, India, Jewish Welfare Association

Johnson, Barbara, essay: "The Cochin Jews of Kerala"

Johnson, Barbara, *Our Community in Two Worlds*

Josephus, Flavius, *Jewish War*, c. 75 CE

Josephus, Flavius, *Antiquities of the Jews*, c. 793 CE

Jussay, P M, *The Jews of Kerala*, India, University of Calicut, 2005

Katz, Nathan and Goldberg, Ellen, *A Jewish King at Shingly*, India, Manohar, 2006

Katz, Nathan and Goldberg, Ellen, *Kashrut, Caste and Kabbalah: The Religious Life of the Jews of Cochin*, India, Manohar, 2005

Katz, Nathan and Goldberg, Ellen, *The Last Jews of Cochin: Jewish Identity in Hindu India*, US, University of South Carolina Press, 1993

Kushner, Gilbert, *Immigrants from India in Israel*, US, University of Arizona Press, 1973

Lawson, Charles Allen, *British and Native Cochin*, UK, Asian Educational Services, 1861

Leviticus, 19:1–2, 11–18

List of rights granted to the Jews of Kerala, engraved upon copper plates presented by the Hindu ruler around 1000 CE. Translated into English from Tamil from a replica of the plates housed in the Israel Museum Collection

Loti, Pierre, *India*, London, Asian Educational Services, Originally published in 1903. Reprinted in 1995

Mandelbaum, David, *The Jewish Way of Life in Cochin*, US, Jewish Social Studies, 1939

Mandelbaum, David, *Society in India*, US, University of California Press, 1970

Mandelbaum, David, *Social Stratification among the Jews of Cochin in India and in Israel*, *Jewish Journal of Sociology*, 1975

Mandelbaum, David, *A Case History of Judaism*: *The Jews of Cochin in India and in Israel*, 1981

Menon, K.P.P., *History of Kerala*, India, 1929

Narayan, G, *Cultural Symbiosis in Kerala*, India, 1972

Nissim, Rabbi, fourteenth century poet and traveler who wrote of the King of Shingly

Pannikkar, K.M., *Malabar and the Portuguese*, India, Voice of India

Pliny the Elder, *Naturalis Historia*

Pliny the Elder, *The Periplus of the Erythraean Sea*

Polo, Marco, *The Travels of Marco Polo, the Venetian*, 1904

Psalm 84:3

Psalm 91

Psalm 144:4

Rabinowitz, Rabbi Louis, *Far East Mission*, Eagle Press, South Africa, 1952

Shilappadikaram, or *Lay of the Ankle Bracelet*, India, second century Tamil poem

Shoskes, Henry, *Your World and Mine*, US, 1947

Edited by Slapek, Orpa, *The Jews of India*, Israel, The Israel Museum, 2003

Talmud, Hagigah 27a

The Chennamangalam Synagogue: A Jewish Community in a Village in Kerala, India

Pamphlet produced by the synagogue

Zimra, Rabbi David ben Solonom ibn, letter to the Cochini Jews from Cairo, 1520